The First Americans

INDIANS OF THE SOUTHWEST

Karen Liptak

Facts On File, Inc.

AN INFOBASE HOLDINGS COMPANY

About *The First Americans* Series:

This eight-volume series presents the rich and varied cultures of the many Native American tribes, placing each within its geographical and historical context. Each volume covers a different cultural area, providing an understanding of all the major North American Indian tribes in a systematic, region-by-region survey. The series emphasizes the contributions of Native Americans to American culture, illustrating their legacy in striking photographs within the text and in all-color photo essays.

Indians of the Southwest

Facts On File, Inc.
11 Penn Plaza
New York, NY 10001

Library of Congress Cataloging-in-Publication Data

Liptak, Karen
    Indians of the Southwest / Karen Liptak
        p.   cm. — The First Americans series
    Includes index.
    Summary: Examines the history, culture, changing fortunes, and
current situation of the various Indian peoples of the Southwest.
    ISBN 0-8160-2385-9
        1. Indians of North America—Southwest, New—Juvenile literature.
    [1. Indians of North America—Southwest, New.]
    I. Title   II. Series.
    E78.S7L58   1991
    979'.00497—dc20   90–45546

Facts On File books are available at special discounts when purchased in bulk quantities for businesses, associations, institutions or sales promotions. Please call our Special Sales Department in New York at 212/967-8800 or 800/322-8755

Design by Carmela Pereira
Jacket design by Donna Sinisgalli
Typography & composition by Tony Meisel

10 9 8 7 6 5 4 3

This book is printed on acid-free paper.
Manufactured in MEXICO.

▲ Zuni Pueblo in New Mexico, photographed in 1879.

CONTENTS

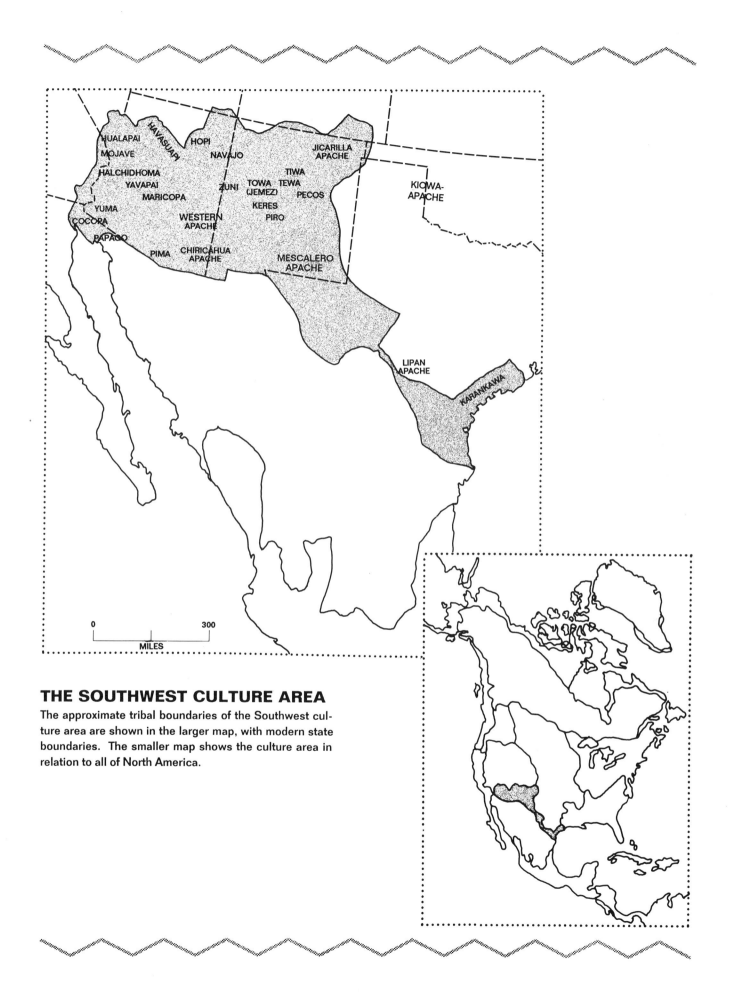

THE SOUTHWEST CULTURE AREA

The approximate tribal boundaries of the Southwest culture area are shown in the larger map, with modern state boundaries. The smaller map shows the culture area in relation to all of North America.

▲ A young Hopi woman wears her hair in the traditional style.

CHAPTER ONE

ROOTS

he Indians of the Southwest developed their unique cultures in a land that today includes Arizona, New Mexico, southwest Colorado, southern Utah, and southwest Nevada, as well as small parts of Texas and Oklahoma, the California border of the Colorado River, and northern Mexico. It is a region of contrasts, with areas as open and beautiful as they are harsh.

The haunting sights in the north include dusty flat-topped mesas, broad valleys, steep-walled canyons and majestic mountains with forests of yellow pine, pinons, and junipers. Brilliant sunrises and sunsets behind rocks sculptured by eons of winds, rains, and erosion create scenes that are unforgettable.

Further south, the flat desert regions are both serene and mysterious, with many bizarre-looking animals and plants that have adapted to the challenge of living in infertile and hostile lands. Here you will find animals like javelinas, gila monsters, desert tortoises, and roadrunners, as well as plants like sagebrush, saguaro, and prickly cacti. In this region of boiling heat during the days and intense cold at night, rain is both precious and potentially dangerous. The desert may lack rainfall for many months, then receive downpours severe enough to cause flooding.

Perhaps it was partly in response to this wild, awe-inspiring, and often inhospitable country that many Indians of the Southwest developed a life-style in which religion was part of everything they did, and sacred rites accompanied almost every activity. They have come to know many natural formations as sacred places, to respect the spirit in every object, and to feel a oneness with a land they recognize as a gift for them to use and protect.

In some areas, Southwestern Indians of today continue to live in many ways as their people did centuries ago. This is especially true in some of the Pueblo villages on the Rio Grande, such as Taos, where time-honored traditions refuse to bow to contemporary influences. At the same time, many Pueblo Indians, like Apache, Navajo, and other Southwestern Indians, are business-people, and more and more youngsters are leaving their pueblos and reservations to study at universities throughout the country.

However, while the many roads taken by Southwestern tribes vary, all share a bond with the home and the spirits of their ancestors. Non-Indian visitors to the Southwest find that Native Americans in this region have many subtle lessons about the world to teach them, and modern Native Americans themselves are gaining a new appreciation for their rich heritage.

ANCIENT PEOPLES

The first known inhabitants of the Southwest are commonly called Paleo-Indians. These ancient people very likely were hunters and gatherers who came across the Bering Strait from Asia during an Ice Age some 10,000 years ago. They probably came in waves, some settling in the area, and others moving toward the east as the big game they relied upon declined in the area.

Later, other early ancestors of the Southwestern Indians were to come up from Mexico in the south, and make the Southwest their new home.

The most noted southern migrants are the ancestors of Arizona's Tohono O'odham. (In 1986, the Papago people chose Tohono O'odham, or Desert People, as their new name. The Spanish name for them—Papago—means "bean eaters," because they ate so many mesquite beans.) These ancient peoples are known by the Pima word Hohokam, which means "those who have gone."

The Hohokam founded a rich culture in southern Arizona. They gathered wild beans and

▲ Acoma Pueblo in New Mexico shown in a 1936 photo by renowned photographer Ansel Adams. Today, Acoma has become more of a ceremonial home, with almost every family having a house or clan home here, and another home in a nearby residential community.

cactus, produced pottery and basketry, and built a deep depression surrounded by ridges that appears to be a large ball court, similar to those found in ruined cities far to the south in Mexico.

The Hohokam appear to have stayed in their Southwestern Salt River and Gila River Valley homes for over 1,500 years. Archaeologists have found evidence that the Hohokam were the first true masters of the desert. They managed to successfully farm the arid lands by digging vast irrigation canals and growing corn and cotton.

One of the most well-known Hohokam ruins is Snaketown, now part of the Pima Indian Gila River Reservation in Arizona. Here, the Hohokam once flooded their fields with water brought from the Gila River three miles away. Here, too, many of the Hohokam's most beautiful artifacts—such

▲ Taos Pueblo, once one of the most isolated of the eastern pueblos, as it looked in 1941.

as stone vessels and clay figurines—were found purposely smashed. This destruction remains an engrossing mystery.

The Hopi and most of the other Pueblo groups, are descended from another group of early people. These are called the Anasazi, which means "the ancient ones" in the Navajo language. The Anasazi, also known as the Basket Makers, lived in the Four Corners Area (where Arizona, New Mexico, Colorado, and Utah meet) from about A.D. 500 to around A.D. 1300. Then they deserted the region for reasons we can only guess. Most experts believe that they were forced to leave because of drought.

The largest early pueblo complex was Pueblo Bonito in Chaco Canyon, New Mexico. Built by the Anasazi sometime between the 10th and 12th century, it had over 800 rooms. These were linked in a huge, five-story, semicircular apartment house. Pueblo Bonito is made of stones that fit together so well that a knife blade can't be wedged between them. Other famous Anasazi ruins are preserved in Mesa Verde National Park in southwestern Colorado.

Migrations from the Four Corners were primarily to the Rio Grande in what is today New Mexico. Other migrations were to Hopi land in Arizona and Zuni land in New Mexico. This is where the Spanish found the Pueblo Indians, and where they still live today.

The Anasazi, whose culture flowered as early as 100 B.C., are noted for their excellent coiled baskets and elaborately woven sandals. They also made robes of fur and many kinds of cord and rope. Later, they made pottery as well as baskets.

At first these people lived in primitive semi-

LANGUAGE GROUPS

The Native Americans of the Southwest culture area spoke languages from five different families:

ATHAPASCAN
Apache
Navajo

KIOWA-TANOAN
Pueblo tribes

PUENUTIAN
Zuni

UTO-AZTECAN
Hopi
Tohono O'odham (Papago)
Pima
Yaqui

YUMAN
Havasupai
Hualapai
Mojave
Yavapai
Yuma

▶ The ruins of the ancient pueblo of Pecos in New Mexico later served as a landmark for settlers traveling along the Santa Fe Trail.

subterranean pit houses. Later the pit houses grew more elaborate. However, by A.D. 700 the Anasazi were building more and more sophisticated above-ground cliff dwellings.

The Zuni, a Pueblo Indian group, are probably the surviving descendants of another early Indian people—the Mogollons, who lived in pit-house villages southeast of the San Francisco Mountains and had a common ancestor to the Hohokam. Both first appeared around 300 B.C.

About A.D. 825 the ancestors of the Apache began leaving their northern Athabascan relatives (identified by their language) in Alaska and Canada and drifting southward. By the late 1600s they were moving over most of the Southwest.

About A.D. 1024 another Athabascan group left its homeland and eventually came to settle in Arizona and New Mexico. These newcomers were the ancestors of the Navajo, who today live in the Four Corners area and elsewhere and are

▲ An 1879 photograph of the Laguna Pueblo, one of New Mexico's two desert pueblos.

▶ The beautiful ruins at Montezuma Castle National Monument in Arizona feature a five-story structure with 20 rooms built by the Sinagua people, believed to be ancestors of the Hopi.

the largest Indian nation in the United States.

The name for the Pueblo Indians comes from the Spanish word for village. When the first Spaniards arrived in the Southwest in 1540, they discovered these cliff-dwelling farmers living in clusters of terraced stone and mud houses. Today, there are 19 Pueblo groups in New Mexico. Except for Zuni, Acoma, and Laguna, the other New Mexican groups are located along the Rio Grande. These include: Cochiti, Isleta, Jemez, Nambe, Picuris, Pojoaque, Sandia, San Felipe,

San Ildefonso, San Juan, Santa Ana, Santa Clara, Santo Domingo, Taos, Tesuque, and Zia.

Acoma and Laguna are located in the desert, like the pueblos of the only Pueblo Indians who live outside of New Mexico. The Hopi and their neighbors, the Tewa-speaking Indians, make their homes in northeastern Arizona. The Hopi villages are located atop three mesas. Theirs is the most arid and harsh of any Pueblo land.

The Hopi followed the Anasazi into Canyon de Chelly in northeastern Arizona. There they learned to farm their desert land. The Hopi village of Oraibi is the oldest continuously inhabited town in the United States and dates back to approximately A.D. 1100.

Each Pueblo village is a separate and distinct unit. The Pueblo groups speak different languages. The main language groups are known as Keresan, Tiwa, Towa, Tewa, Hopi, and Zunian.

APACHE AND NAVAJO

The word Apache has been attributed to several sources, including a Zuni Indian word meaning strangers. These hunters and gatherers were divided into six distinct divisions, which in turn were divided into bands, each composed of extremely independent people. (Some people consider the Navajo a seventh division of the Apache, since the Navajo and Apache were once a single group united by language and culture. Today the two groups can understand each other's native tongue.)

The six divisions were the Western Apache, Chiricahua, Mescalero, Lipan, Jicarilla, and Kiowa-Apache. We don't know when these Southern Athabascans separated into seven divisions. Today we divide the Apache into two main groups—western and eastern. The western group contains the Western Apache, Chiricahua, and Mescalero. The eastern group contains the Jicarilla, Lipan, and Kiowa-Apache.

All Apache tribes or groupings shared a common language. However, their cultural traits varied from band to band, and depended greatly upon the region they lived in and the people with whom they came into contact.

In the early days, the Western Apache lived in eastern Arizona, from Flagstaff in the north to the Rincon Mountains in the south. These people farmed extensively and were closely linked in language and customs to the Navajo. The Chiricahua, who primarily lived in southeastern Arizona and western New Mexico, were considered the most fierce of the Apache groups. The Mescalero (named by the Spaniards for the mescal or agave plant they gathered) occupied southern New Mexico, east of the Rio Grande. They lived by hunting, gathering, and raiding.

The Jicarilla, who lived in parts of the Four Corners Area, were buffalo hunters, like Indians of the Plains. They also took up farming. The Lipan and Kiowa-Apache lived on the Plains: the Lipan in parts of Texas, and the Kiowa-Apache in areas of Kansas and Oklahoma. Like the Mescalero, these groups engaged in hunting, gathering, and raiding.

The Apache are among the most well-known American Indians. They were both feared and admired for their skill and daring in warfare and raiding. Their warriors were reported to be the most cunning and ingenious in all the land. From childhood, both boys and girls were trained to develop their keen senses and survival skills in battle.

At the same time, the Apache had a strong moral and religious life with a great sense of compassion for their own communities, and exceptionally high regard for their women.

The Navajo, the last Indians to come to the Southwest from the north, shared a similar lifestyle to the Apache. Like many of the Apache groups, they, too, were hunters and gatherers. At times they raided the villages of other Indian tribes, especially the Pueblo, from whom they also learned very much. This included knowledge of raising corn and weaving rugs. When the Spanish came, the Navajo, like the Apache, raided them for their horses. However, unlike the Apache, many Navajo settled down to become sheepherders and farmers.

Like the Pueblo Indians, the Tohono O'odham and Pima were farmers. The Tohono O'odham are very closely related in customs to the Pima who live north of them along the Gila River in south-central Arizona. Both groups speak a Piman language of the Uto-Aztecan language family. (Hopi is another branch of this language group.) The Pima were able to irrigate their fields with water from the Gila and Salt rivers, and they grew many crops in their fields. Like the Tohono O'odham, the Pima hunted in the winter. However, the Tohono O'odham had no permanent river on their land, and as a consequence were much more dependent than the Pima on wild plants and animals.

The Tohono O'odham had a winter home near a spring in the mountains. In the summer the

Tohono O'odham would move down to the valleys, where they stayed while the heavy summer rains fell. When the rains stopped, the people moved back to their winter homes. The Tohono O'odham and Pima were basically peaceful people. When they did go to war, it was generally in defense against more aggressive Indian tribes.

Before the European settlers came, there were seven Indian tribes who spoke dialects of the Yuman language living in the valley of the Colorado River in western and northwestern Arizona. The Lower Colorado River Yuman, including the Yuma (or Quechan, as they call themselves), Maricopa, Mohave, and Cocopa, were farmers who cultivated corn, squash, and beans in fields annually flooded by the Colorado River.

These tribes were completely dependent on the cycles of the seasons, as they had developed no methods of irrigation. Thus, when the spring floods came they left the flood plains for higher ground and stayed there until the water drained from the fields. The Lower Colorado River Yuman were known to have fought among themselves, as well as with Pima, Tohono O'odham,

and Paiute, who lived on the northern border of the Southwest. The Maricopa were aided by the Pima in their fights against both the Mohave and Yuma.

Three other Yuman-speaking tribes living in northern Arizona were primarily hunters and gatherers. These were the "Pai" tribes (*pai* means people), also known as the Upland Yuman. Like most other Yuman, the Havasupai (who were also farmers), their close neighbors, the Hualapai (formerly called the Walapai), and the Yavapai based everything they did on their interpretations of their dreams.

The Havasupai's name means "the people who live at the place which is green." This reflects the place where they have dwelt for centuries—Cataract Canyon, which is a beautiful side branch of the Grand Canyon in northwestern Arizona. Their fertile home is hidden 3,000 feet below the canyon's rim and includes five waterfalls.

The Hualapai are the "Pine People," since they live among the pines. Yavapai means "people of the sun." The Yavapai were once an aggressive

LIFE IN A PUEBLO

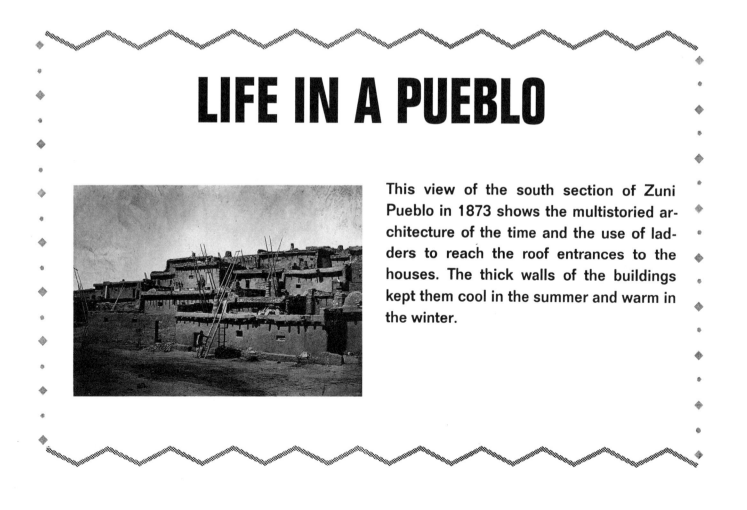

This view of the south section of Zuni Pueblo in 1873 shows the multistoried architecture of the time and the use of ladders to reach the roof entrances to the houses. The thick walls of the buildings kept them cool in the summer and warm in the winter.

group who eventually allied with the Apache and fought many other Indians, including the Havasupai.

All three Pai tribes are noted for their relatively easy, relaxed life-style with little formal organization and their intense individualism.

The Yaqui Indians speak a dialect of Cahita, a language grouping that is part of the Uto-Aztecan language family. The Yaqui were once considered great warriors in their Mexican homeland: they defeated a 16th-century Spanish military expedition trying to enslave them and take their fertile land. They are a recent arrival in the United States, having come to Arizona as refugees from the Yaqui River Valley of Sonora, Mexico, before the turn of the 20th century. They were fleeing from persecution by the Mexican government, which was deporting them to the Yucatan to work as slaves.

In 1978, President Jimmy Carter signed a bill giving the Yaqui full tribal status. This allowed the Yaqui to receive many federal benefits. Today, most Yaqui in the United States live on a section of land at the edge of the Tohono O'odham Reservation near Tucson. Other Yaqui villages exist near Phoenix and in South Tucson.

THE ROOTS OF THE PEOPLE

THE SOUTHWESTERN LANDSCAPE

▲ A rainbow forms over the mountains of Canyonlands National Park in Utah after a rare rainstorm in the desert.

◄ A Navajo sheepherder moves his flock across the arid landscape of Monument Valley in Arizona—much as his ancestors did centuries ago.

▲ Coal Mine Canyon, on the western boundary between the Hopi and Navajo reservations in Arizona, is wild and rugged terrain. Although this land seems inhospitable, the Native Americans of the Southwest lived successfully and harmoniously on it.

▶ Havasu Falls on the Havasupai River in northern Arizona is a beautiful, green oasis. The river is named for the Havasupai, who live in nearby Cataract Canyon.

THE ANCIENT ONES

◀ Cliff Palace, with its elaborate towers and kivas, is Mesa Verde National Park's best known cliff dwelling. This national park, located in Four Corners country, is included on the United Nations' list of the world's greatest natural wonders.

◀ Visitors must climb a very high ladder to reach the secluded and well-protected site of Balcony House in Mesa Verde National Park, Colorado. It is built in a picturesque cave 700 feet above the canyon floor.

▼ Sun Temple, a building located atop the mesa across the canyon from Cliff Palace in Mesa Verde National Park, is believed to have been a religious structure.

▲ The Wupatki ruins near Flagstaff, Arizona, are remains of an ancient Paleo-Indian ceremonial center. These people, the ancestors of the Hopi, built their complex homes entirely by hand: they had no horses or other beasts of burden to help carry the stones.

▶ Part of Chaco Culture National Historical Park in New Mexico, Pueblo Bonito is a gigantic ruin that contains over 800 rooms.

◀ The well-preserved buildings at Gila Cliff Dwellings National Monument are sheltered in natural cavities on the face of an overhanging cliff in New Mexico. The site was inhabited from about 1280 to the early 1300s.

▲ The White House ruin in Canyon de Chelly National
Monument, now part of the Navajo Nation in Arizona.

LIVING

The earliest inhabitants of the Southwest lived in semi-underground pit dwellings. Later, the Anasazi began building their multistory stone and adobe structures. Some Pueblo Indians still live in such housing, as at Taos, but more often these have been replaced by single-family dwellings made from cinder blocks. In other pueblos, the multistory structures that remain are now used as centers of worship, rather than as living quarters.

In most Pueblo villages, house building was primarily women's work. The walls of early Pueblo homes were made from adobe (clay that has dried) or stone. Each family's dwelling was in an apartment house of one to six stories.

The roofs were made of peeled cottonwood logs, willow rods, grass, and brush, all covered with adobe. The roof of one story became the floor of the next story.

To protect themselves against enemies, the lower story of the pueblo was built without windows or doors. It was entered through a hole in the roof that also let the smoke from indoor fires escape. This entrance hole was reached by a ladder that could be pulled up quickly in case of attack. Another ladder was used to climb down into the rooms. Higher stories had small openings in the walls that served as windows.

A unique feature of Pueblo villages are the rooms known as kivas. A kiva is an underground ceremonial chamber in which men meet and boys learn the traditions of their tribes. Although women build the homes, the kivas are off limits to them. These are generally built by the men who are members of the secret society to which each kiva belongs. Some kivas are free-standing, others attached to apartments.

The Eastern Apache lived in tipis: oval-shaped dwellings made of poles covered with animal skin. These homes were similar to those of the Plains Indians and could be packed-up and carried by dog (or later by horse) when the Apache band moved on.

Other groups of these people lived in communities of wickiups. Wickiups are made of poles that are cross-tied with branches and covered with grass and brush. Unlike the tipis, the wickiups were burned before their builders traveled from one campsite to another.

During most of the year, the Navajo lived in hogans. These are domed circular structures framed with wood and covered with mud and clay. In the summer, the Navajo built temporary shelters that had roofs made of brush but were open on all four sides.

Tohono O'odham houses were dome-shaped structures, with their floors beneath ground level. They were made from bent rods of wood that were covered with brush and mud. The door was usually so small that one had to crawl through it. A family would have a community of houses all together, for the parents and the families of their married sons. The houses shared an outdoor cooking area, where the women all prepared food together. Tohono O'odham homes were similar in shape to Pima houses, although the materials and size of the two differed. The Tohono O'odham used supports of cottonwood and giant cactus, while the Pima used willow and mesquite.

LIFE-STYLES AND LIFEWAYS

Throughout the Southwest, the family was very close-knit in the Indian cultures. The tribes felt great respect and gave thanks, not only for the land, but for other members of the family and the community. But each group had its own unique religious, social, and political structures. Taken together, these three factors are known as a tribe's lifeway.

Some of the Pueblo villages, like the Hopi, have a clan system with the clan mother at its head. Another basic Pueblo social structure is the moiety, a division of a group into two parts. Such divisions are usually for social, ceremonial, and political reasons.

Pueblo clans are formed from related families, with the children belonging to their mother's clan. While members of the same clan cannot marry, the Pueblo Indians encourage marriage within the same village. The clans are named for

▲ A Havasupai woman outside her thatch-roofed winter home.

the ancestors of their members.

Among the Zuni, there are 13 or more clans, with names such as the Bear Clan, the Corn Clan, the Eagle Clan, and the Sun Clan.

In early days, Pueblo Indian men owned no property. The fields belonged to various clans and were subdivided into separate family property owned by the women. The women owned the herds, flocks, and crops, as well as the household goods and the house itself. The chiefs inherited their offices and the right to ceremonial properties and rituals through their mothers. When a Pueblo man married, he left his childhood home and went to live in his wife's house.

Today, as in the past, each Rio Grande pueblo is led by a cacique, a spiritual leader who is responsible for legislating laws. The cacique, chosen for life, has a war chief, who like him is believed to be guided by the Great Spirit.

The war chief has assistants: the people who enforce the laws set into motion by the cacique. Under the war chief is the war captain and his assistants, who are responsible for the well-being of the animals in the pueblo. These positions are filled each year, with selections made by the cacique, his staff, pueblo society chiefs and the war chief. There is also a lieutenant war captain and his aides, selected to police the pueblo for a one-year term. The war captain and his aides are chosen from a different moiety each year.

After the Spanish arrival in the Southwest, the office of pueblo governor was created. The governor of each pueblo is under the cacique's supervision and responsible for all the tribal dealings with the outside world. There is also a tribal council, which in most villages is made up of previous governors of the village.

As in the past, today the Navajo and Western

▲ The interior of a Navajo hogan in New Mexico, taken in 1903. Today the hogan might have electricity and a television, but would otherwise look much the same.

Apache belong to clans. Every Navajo and Western Apache child is born into the clan of his or her mother, and the clans regulate marriage.

In the past, when an Apache man married he went to live with his wife's family and helped provide for them. However, although he built his home near his mother-in-law, and he even supported her, he was not permitted to speak to her or even be in the same wickiup as her.

The Navajo also had a mother-in-law taboo, although the origin of this custom is not known. Another Navajo custom was for men to marry more than one woman: preferably two sisters. This was considered a way of keeping extended families together. Several groups of extended families would live together and form a community that used the common land.

Until the beginning of the 20th century, the Navajo were arranged into loosely defined local groups led by a local leader. The leaders of such groups came together to negotiate and sign peace treaties. It has been reported that the Navajo once had 12 war chiefs and 12 peace chiefs, but very little is known about them and this system.

The Apache lacked a central tribal government. Bands within each tribe were made up of a number of extended families that loosely controlled a region and each had a leader, generally the most dynamic family headman.

In contrast to the Pueblo, Navajo, and Apache, among the Tohono O'odham and Pima descent was through the father. The people were divided into clans, with women belonging to the clan on their father's side. The Tohono O'odham had two main clans, the Buzzard and the Coyote. Houses of extended families were grouped into villages.

Until the United States became involved in Tohono O'odham affairs, their villages existed without a single leader in the western sense. However, each village had a ceremonial house

▲ A Zuni cacique named Paliwahtiwa was photographed in the 1880s.

that functioned much like the Pueblo kiva. Men met there to settle their problems at meetings led by the Keeper of the Smoke, who lit the fire in the settlement's central fireplace. He was also in charge of community ceremonies. There were other leaders for war parties and for deer and rabbit hunts. However, the word of the leader was not absolute. Decisions were not final unless every man in the council over the age of 30 was in agreement.

The Pima had four clans and these clans regulated village activities, including marriage. Each village had a leader who settled arguments, chose the times and places for ceremonies, conducted meetings, and kept the village's sacred objects safe.

The Havasupai and other Pai people were noticeably lacking in formal tribal organizations, such as clans or moieties. Their unit of society was solely the family, either nuclear or extended. Certain individuals were considered tribal chiefs, but they lacked real authority. Their leadership was limited to giving advice or being persuasive and was inherited through the father, although a

successor could be passed over if he was deemed to be unworthy of the honor. To be worthy one had to be wise and brave, as well as very even-tempered. There were seldom council meetings called; issues got resolved as the men took their sweat baths in the sweat lodge.

CLOTHING

Before European explorers arrived, many Indians in the Southwest wore clothing made from either animal skins or cotton woven on a type of loom. On their feet they wore either sandals or moccasins. Some form of jewelry was worn by all the tribes, and the distinctive hairstyles of the various tribes were a part of their attire.

Pueblo men often wore cotton shirts; these were frequently embroidered. For special occasions, they put on their special fringed animal skin shirts.

The Hopi men were fond of loose-fitting white cotton trousers. Other Pueblo men wore cotton kilts or broad sashes and breechcloths. For ceremonies, the kilts were embroidered or brocaded. At one time, Pueblo men wore animal skin robes that were tied together with cord from the yucca cactus. Later, the Spanish arrived with woolen blankets to trade, and these replaced earlier animal garments.

The blankets that Pueblo women draped around their bodies to wear as dresses were known as mantas. A cotton belt and shawl were two additional pieces of clothing.

During bad weather, moccasins were worn in the Pueblo villages. These shoes had soft buckskin tops and hard rawhide soles. Everyday moccasins were generally red or black, although blue moccasins were used in some ceremonial dances. Married women could be told apart from those who were unmarried by their moccasins: single women had wraparound moccasin boots, while married women had loosely fitting ones.

The Apache primarily wore clothing made from animal skins: skirts for the women and breechcloths for the men. Their distinctive knee-high moccasins were folded at the top and could hold small objects. The toes were upturned for added protection against the rough terrain.

The earliest clothes of the Navajo were made from grass and yucca. Later, when the Navajo began trading with the Ute of Colorado they obtained buckskins from which they started making shirts, moccasins, dresses, and leggings. Navajo women wore fringed dresses made out of two

▲ In this 1890 photo, a woman from Isleta Pueblo is shown carrying a baby wrapped in a blanket, or manta, on her back.

pieces of skin that were laced together at the sides. Buckskin thongs held the dress up and a cape made from buckskin was worn over it.

Navajo men wore moccasins that were stained red, wrapped around the ankle and fastened with silver buttons.

In the 1600s, as they became more and more influenced by the Pueblo culture, the Navajo began wearing Pueblo-style woollen blankets, and cotton clothing. In the late 1800s women wore velveteen blouses and long skirts like those popular in Europe. At that time men wore velveteen shirts and white cotton trousers.

Tohono O'odham women wore skirts made from cotton or buckskin, while Tohono O'odham men wore cotton or buckskin breechcloths. Instead of moccasins, the Tohono O'odham wore sandals made from twisted string or mountain sheep skin.

Tohono O'odham women had blue lines tattooed on their faces from the chin to the mouth. Tattooing was done with cactus thorn. Although the process was painful, women in their teens were expected to have it done. The Lower Col-

HAIRSTYLES

Many Pueblo men tied a folded headband around the forehead, braided their hair, and held it in place with a white cord. Others wore their hair tied at the nape of the neck in the traditional hourglass style known as the chango. The Navajo and some Apache tribes also wore their hair in this distinctive way. Both men and women generally preferred wearing their hair long, although Hopi men wore a unique short pageboy.

Young, unmarried Hopi maidens had one of the most unusual hairstyles in the region. They put their hair up to represent either the squash blossom or a butterfly's wings. These were called butterfly whorls.

orado River tribes also tattooed their faces, and liberally painted their faces and bodies also.

LIVING OFF THE LAND

Corn (maize), beans, and squash were the most important cultivated foods of the Southwestern Indians. Cotton, gourds, and tobacco were also grown by these Native Americans who felt a strong bond with the earth. They did not plant or harvest crops, or gather wild plants, without the appropriate prayers and offerings.

Water was the crucial factor in Southwestern agriculture since so much of the land was arid. There were droughts to worry about, as well as flooding. In some cases, the solution to the water problem was to plant crops in flood plains, and then wait for the annual or biannual floods to water them. A more productive technique was to control the flooding with dikes or dams.

Irrigation ditches were also built. These brought water from the rivers to the dry land. Water was also carried to the fields in jars.

Corn was the staple food of the Pueblo Indians. The Hopi, who grow different varieties of it, say that they have been able to live on their arid land for centuries without irrigation by singing, talking, and praying to their corn. Today, as in the past, they use a simple wooden digging stick to push away the dry surface until they get to the moist ground underneath. There they plant their seeds: always more than enough kernels of corn in each hole.

Corn is also very important to the Apache, who associate it with the Gan, or Mountain Spirits. Some Apache tribes say that they obtained corn from their Hopi friends and Pima enemies. Other Apache believe that corn came from Mexicans and Pueblo.

While the women tend the crops among the Apache, the men do the farming among the Pueblo. However, throughout the Southwest, it was the woman's task to grind the corn. This was done with sets of stones, consisting of a cylindrical mano, and a larger, flat metate.

Piki bread continues to be the most important staple for the Hopi. The women mix blue cornmeal with boiling water to make the batter. Then, after lightly greasing a stone griddle with toasted squash seeds, they use their fingers to delicately spread a thin layer of batter over it. In seconds the bread is cooked and ready to be rolled up and served. As the rolls cool they become crisp.

Corn is also boiled or roasted on the cob. The

▲ A Pueblo man from the Acoma Pueblo, photographed in the early part of the 20th century. He wears a blanket as a shawl.

Indian green corn is like the familiar corn on the cob of today. It is usually left in the husk and roasted in a fire, a pit, or an oven. It is also dried in the sun and stripped from the cobs.

Another method of preparing corn is to steam-bake it. When the Apache cook it in this way, they place wood in a pit, place rocks on it, and then light the pit with a ritual for the occasion. After the pit is hot, the smoldering wood is removed, corn stalks are laid on the hot stones, and then many ears of corn, husked or unhusked, are thrown into the pit. These are covered with corn stalks. Then the whole pit is covered with dirt. A stick that was left in the pit is then removed through the earth. This leaves a hole through which water is poured into the pit to steam the corn. Then the opening is covered with dirt, and the pit is left alone for one night. Next morning, it is removed and cooled.

Ground corn can be eaten plain, mixed with other ground seeds and eaten, or cooked into a mush or gruel. Cornmeal dumplings are made by

▲ Before an unmarried Hopi female could wear the double whorl hairdo shown here, she had to prove her mastery of the skill of grinding corn.

▲ Both Hopi men and women wore elaborate hairstyles. In this picture a Hopi man has his hair dressed by his wife.

rolling a mixture of corn and water into balls, and dropping them into boiling water. Tortillas are made by spreading a cornmeal batter on a hot stone griddle. Today, as in the past, blue corn is favored for tortillas, though white corn is used and also considered good.

Corn was made into drinks, as well as food. These included pinole, which was popular among travelers. Pinole was made by grinding roasted dry corn into a powder, then mixing it with cold water. Beer was also made from corn.

Corn could be used for more than food and drink: small corn stalks were made into bedding material; Southwestern Indians used cobs to make pipe bowls; and some curved ears of corn were used in curing rituals by medicine men.

Throughout the Southwest, corn pollen was considered sacred. Today it continues to be used in many spiritual ceremonies. It is often sprinkled on participants and on the ground. Sometimes it is mixed with cattail pollen, a bright yellow powder also considered holy.

A variety of beans was cultivated by Indians of the Southwest. Many kinds could be planted at the same time, irrigated in the same way, and harvested together. The Apache generally planted their beans in the early spring, at the same time that they planted corn. Later in the season, the beans were harvested along with the corn crop. Beans, as well as squash, were usually planted between the corn.

When dried corn and beans were boiled together, sometimes with meat, they formed a dish that we call succotash.

Squash was prepared by peeling the plant, cutting it in half, and then sun-drying it. The squash seeds were roasted and eaten whole. They were also crushed to make an oil that was used to grease griddles. The flowers were sometimes cooked.

In many areas, smoking tobacco was considered an essential part of ceremonies and meetings. Most tribes in the Southwest gathered wild tobacco, which was very strong (the Havasupai mixed their supply with bear grease to provide a milder smoke).

However, the Tohono O'odham and Pima learned how to cultivate tobacco as a crop. They believed that cultivated tobacco was too shy to grow near people. Therefore, it was planted far from the village. The leaves were dried and kept for smoking on special occasions, but unlike most other North American Indians, the Tohono O'odham did not use pipes. Instead, they smoked their tobacco in pieces of hollow reeds or the inner sheath of corn.

Cotton has been grown for cloth in the Southwest at least since the Hohokam Indians culti-

vated it in their irrigated fields as early as A.D. 300, and possibly earlier.

The Pueblo Indians, as well as the Pima and Tohono O'odham, used cotton for clothing as well as for string. However, the Tohono O'odham region was too dry to produce a substantial crop of cotton. They got their supply through trade with the Pima, who lived near water.

In the Southwest, cotton was harvested in the fall, with the seeds usually hand-picked from the fiber. Bundles of fiber were brushed, and then spun with a spindle that measured about one to two feet long. The spindle consisted of a rod with a disk about a third of the way from the bottom. After the fiber was spun, it was woven on a loom, and a wooden comb was used to even up the stitches.

WILD FOODS

The acorn was an important plant in the Southwest, especially among most of the Western Apache bands. They used long straight poles to knock the acorns down from the oak trees during gathering trips.

Although some kinds of acorns could be eaten whole and raw, most were ground up for use. Acorn flour could be eaten dry or moistened, as well as sprinkled on foods, or pounded into meats. It could also be mixed with soups.

Whole acorns could be boiled, and acorn bread was made by mixing acorn meal with wheat flour. Uncooked acorn meal was served in a Western Apache meat stew, a favorite dish.

Known as mescal and century plant, agave was the most important wild food plant to many Southwestern people, including the Apache.

Life was often sustained for many weeks at a time by the agave, a plant of many uses. The plant's crown is edible, and its juice can be fermented into a drink. The flowers can also be made into a beverage. The agave thorn becomes a needle, as well as thread, and the stalk can be transformed into the shaft for a spear. It can be made into a fiddle, with which young Apache men serenaded women.

Apache groups customarily waited until after the corn harvest before they prepared agave for the winter. They traveled in groups to where the agave grew, having selected the best plants during the previous fall.

The women were in charge of gathering and preparing agave. Groups of women selected a roasting place, then set out to find suitable

▲ Four women from the Keresan-speaking pueblo of Acoma with decorated water jugs. All water for drinking, cooking, and irrigation had to be carried by hand.

plants. They used an agave chisel and knife to cut or pry loose the plant, trimming its leaves with the knife.

While the women gathered the plants, the men prepared a roasting pit. They filled their pit with wood, over which a layer of stones were placed. Then the fire pit was lit with a sunrise ritual performed by a man or woman who was considered a lucky person.

The fire continued to burn until there was no more fuel. Now brush, or grass, was quickly thrown over the hot stones, and the agave crowns placed on top. Each woman had a way of identifying which agave—some weighing as much as 20 pounds each—belonged to her. Additional layers of vegetation were placed over the crowns. Then the entire pit was covered with dirt. Cooking the agave took two days. Finally, the pit was uncovered, and the agave removed.

The heart of the crown was the sweetest part of the plant. It was usually saved as a candy for boys and girls. The agave flower stalk was baked when relatively young, and chewed for juice. Agave served a variety of nonfood purposes, too. Parts of it were made into detergents, cheek blush, paints, and spear shafts.

The desert tribes were especially well acquainted with the virtues of cacti. During today's hot summer months, the Pima and Tohono O'odham still harvest the sweet red fruit of the

▲ A Navajo hogan and cornfield near Holbrook, Arizona, photographed in 1889. Even though the land is dry, the corn grows well.

saguaro with long poles made from saguaro ribs. (The poles are also good for harvesting the beans of the mesquite tree.)

Saguaro fruit can be eaten raw. It can also be made into dried fruit cakes. The Pima and Tohono O'odham boil the fruit into a syrup, then store it for the winter. The Tohono O'odham give a portion of each family's syrup to the rainmaking camp, where the sacred wine is made. This fermented drink is shared at the annual saguaro wine feast, an important rain-making ceremony. Saguaro seeds are eaten, too. They can be roasted, then ground, mixed with water, and served as mush.

Other kinds of cacti are currently used, as they were in days past, for both food and healing purposes. The fruit of the prickly pear is peeled and eaten raw, and also made into a type of jam. The Indians living in the desert climate know just when the prickly pear fruit will ripen and fall. Thus, they make sure to gather it before the wild animals have a chance to eat it.

Mesquite was another rich supply of food in the desert. After the small tree ripened in late summer its pods were gathered, dried in the sun, and pounded into a sweet-tasting flour. Mesquite flour was stored by wetting it so that it hardened into a long-lasting cake.

The pounded pulp of fresh mesquite beans was squeezed to make a juice. Another drink was made by mixing the flour with warm water.

Stored dried beans of the mesquite were chewed, and the pulp and seeds spit out. Children enjoyed chewing mesquite pitch as a kind of gum. It was also used as a glue to attach arrow points to shafts, and as the foundation for a beauty treatment. After being scraped off with a

▲ From June to mid-July, Pima women harvest the ripe red fruit of the saguaro by knocking it to the ground with long poles.

sharp stone ax and dried, the pitch was pounded into a powder and mixed with sticky black mud. The result was a mud pack that both sexes used on their black hair to make it more lustrous.

Yucca is the name given to a group of shrubs or trees of the agave family, which have bell-shaped flowers when in bloom. It produces a fleshy fruit that can be picked when green, then ripened, cooked, and dried for winter. Yucca roots were made into soaps, molasses, and laxatives. The Hopi and other Pueblo people used the suds from yucca root in their ceremonies.

The leaves of this versatile plant provided threads in a variety of textures from which such items as blankets, sandals, and paint brushes were made. Yucca leaves were used in Indian basketry, and yucca pitch was used to waterproof many baskets.

There were many other wild plants that added diversity to the diet of the Southwestern Indians. One of the most popular was the nut of the pinon pine. The nuts were gathered by shaking the tree, or by simply picking up nuts that fell to the ground. The nuts were eaten by themselves, or mixed with baked yucca fruit. They also could be ground fine in their shells, and blended with other foods, such as agave and berries.

Another very useful wild plant in the Southwest was cattail, which provided food, as well as material for mats, baskets, cradles, and rope.

The flowering head of the cattail produces a brilliant yellow pollen for about one week each year. This was used for bread or mush by some groups; and the roots were cooked by steaming in a pit, or roasting over an open fire.

COOKING

Pit-cooking was a common method of cooking. A pit was dug, and lined with stones. Then a fire was started over the stones. When the fire became red-hot the wood and ashes were removed, and the food was added, often wrapped in corn husks or various plant leaves. Food could be steam-cooked in a pit if a stick was planted in the center of the pit, then removed after the pit was covered with dirt, allowing for a hole through which water could be added.

HUNTING

There were both large and small animals to be hunted by Indians of the Southwest. Deer were especially important to them. Hopi hunters armed with bows and arrows formed a large circle around the deer when they were feeding. By only moving when the deer were busy eating, the men could sneak up on their prey. Then a few of the men quietly walked into the center of the circle and slowly forced the deer toward the waiting hunters.

Another common method of hunting deer was to set fire to the grass surrounding the deer. The frightened animals would huddle in the center of the circle and be easily caught by the hunters. Pitfalls were also used. The Navajo would dig several pits along deer trails, and cover them with vegetation. Then they drove the deer toward the pits. Sometimes the pits were left alone, but checked daily for any game that might have fallen in.

Many deer hunters wore disguises to fool the deer. The Navajo dressed in the head and neck of the deer. They had thongs attached to their costume that they worked to make the fake deer's

▲ A crop of pumpkins is seen growing near a single-family Zuni adobe, around 1897. Pumpkins and other squash are important foods for the Pueblo people.

ears wiggle. Some disguises were so realistic that there are cases on record where hunters were known to have shot each other by mistake.

The antelope was another animal hunted in the Southwest. The Navajo tracked them to exhaustion by setting up a kind of relay system of men. One man would chase the antelope until he reached the next man, who would take over the chase until he came to a third man, and so on until the antelope was too tired to escape.

Other big animal game included the mountain sheep and the buffalo. The powerful buffalo was hunted by the Apache on the Plains, as well as by the eastern Pueblo. Buffalo were shot by bow and arrow when they came to drink at water holes. They were also chased to exhaustion, driven over a cliff or into a corral, and encircled by a ring of fire.

Small game were also hunted by the Southwestern Indians. Rabbits were the main source of fresh meat for many tribes, including the Hopi. Catching them was often a community affair. In some groups, the hunters walked toward the animals in a straight line, throwing curved sticks at the animals as they tried to get away.

Nets were also used for catching rabbits. In earlier days, these were made from brush. Later, nets were woven from strong cotton cord. The rabbits were driven into the nets by a circle of hunters, who then used throwing sticks to kill the animals. Since the sticks bounced, a hunter could sometimes hit more than one rabbit with a single throw.

When the Hopi were hunting rabbit meat for everyday use, women could accompany the men on their hunts. However, when the Hopi were

▲ Two women from the Taos Pueblo, New Mexico, bake bread in an wood-burning outdoor stone oven in 1916. Scenes almost exactly like this can still be seen at Taos Pueblo today.

hunting rabbit meat for ceremonial use, only men were allowed along. The group always included the medicine man, who made offerings to the spirits of the rabbits. Just as they do today, the Hopi would politely tell the rabbits that they were put on Earth to provide food for the people. Then they asked the animals' forgiveness before they killed them.

Traps were used throughout the Southwest: their main feature was that they would work in the absence of a hunter. The two traps used most often were the deadfall and the snare. A deadfall works by crushing an animal under a heavy weight, either a stone or a log, as the animal goes after the bait. A snare uses a noose for catching an animal.

Small deadfalls were used for trapping prairie dogs, which live in underground "towns" containing hundreds of animals. Prairie dogs were also dug out of their burrows, or shot with a bow and arrow. A trick used by the Navajo was to set up a sheet of mica in front of the burrow. Since mica reflected sunlight into the burrow, the prairie dog would be blinded as it exited its hole, and captured with ease.

Animals were hunted for food and more. They provided the sinew needed to make equipment, such as thread and bowstrings. Animal skins were used for clothing and drums. Indians made tools from animal bone and some tribes used animal hoofs for ceremonial rattles.

Meat was preserved by drying it in the sun, and then cutting it into strips. The resulting product was known as jerky. This food kept for a few weeks and could be taken along on trips.

The bow and arrow was the most common hunting equipment in the Southwest. Almost any kind of wood was used to make bows. The bows were usually created from saplings (young trees) that were about three inches thick. The sapling was split in half, and the inner side of the wood became the belly of the bow. The wood was scraped, then carefully bent. A notch or two was cut into each end to hold the bow string. The bow was rubbed with animal fat to keep it from cracking by drying too soon. Then it was left to dry for a few months. When it was ready to use, a bowstring was attached. The most often used bowstring material was sinew.

The art of making arrows required great skill. Arrow shafts were created from the shoots of practically any tree. The shoots were peeled, then tied in bundles to straighten them. Like the bow wood, the bundles of shoots were left to dry for a few months. Then they were straightened some more over a fire and bent into shape.

Feathers were attached to the arrow shafts to help direct their flight. These came from the wings or tails of large birds, such as turkeys or crows. Strands of sinew were used to bind the feathering to the arrow.

Arrowheads were made of many materials, primarily stone or bone. Soapweed, a form of yucca, was also used. The arrowhead was fastened on with wet sinew, which would shrink as it dried, and hold the arrowhead firmly.

Arrows were carried, with their points facing down, in a carrier known as a quiver. This was usually made from buckskin or rawhide.

Perhaps the best fisherpeople of the Southwest were the Lower Colorado River Yuman, including the Maricopa and Mohave. Both of these tribes fished with fish scoops made from willow. Young boys used long fishing poles to which they attached cotton lines. They made their hooks from the curved spines of barrel cactus.

Fish were generally eaten fresh, rather than dried. Among the Yuman tribes, it was customarily the man's job to cook the fish, which they either broiled or boiled with finely ground corn.

TOYS AND GAMES

Recreation was an important part of Southwest Indian life for every age group. Such activities as chasing butterflies and birds are universal parts of being young. Indian children enjoyed these pastimes, just as children do today. But they also had special toys and games.

Tops were favorites of the Hopi children. The men of the tribe made them; the girls' tops were plain, while the boys' tops were painted with bands of red, white, or black. But the Hopi could only play with this toy at certain times. The top's humming noise sounded like the wind, which tops were believed to bring. After early spring, the toys had to be put away, because wind storms could destroy the newly growing plants.

The bull-roarer, also known as the whizzing stick, was another noisy toy. It was basically a thin piece of wood with a long cord attached to one end. When the wood was quickly whirled around the head, it made a distinctive roar. The Navajo heard in it the sound of the thunderbird, whose flapping was believed to bring the thunder. The thunderbird was also thought to make lightning, and bull-roarers often had lightning symbols painted on them. As with tops, children could not play with bull-roarers any later than early spring.

The whirligig was a similar toy. It consisted of a flat piece of pottery, or stone with one or more cords attached on either side. Pulling on the cords forced the disks to whirl around. Early versions of this toy have been found in prehistoric Southwestern cliff dwellings.

Southwestern Indian boys and girls also loved playing games. Older Hopi boys enjoyed a nighttime game called the witch game. The player picked to be the witch was given a small drum. Then he had to hide and let the others try to find him. If they headed-off in the wrong direction, the witch beat upon his drum, then quickly ran to another secret spot.

Maricopa Indian boys enjoyed a good mud fight. This was a team sport. It began with each team member holding a huge hunk of mud and a stick. One by one, they plopped a small glob of mud on the end of the stick and threw the mud at the other team. The boys would try to duck, while keeping their line intact. The losing team was the side that broke ranks first.

Games of chance were widely played in the Southwest, mainly by adults, and betting was expected. Among the Apache, secret ceremonies were held to bring players good luck before they played these games. One game of chance was the hidden-ball game. Two sides played against each other in this game. A person from one side hid an object. A person from the other guessed its lo-

▲ In 1868 the Navajo of Canyon de Chelly, shown above, were relocated by the United States to New Mexico. They eventually returned to live at the bottom of the same canyon the Anasazi once occupied.

cation. The hider tried to confuse the opponent, and then had to keep a poker face so as not to reveal the secret.

Another widespread Indian guessing game was the hand game. A player began by holding two small wooden cylinders: one was plain, the other was not. The player's opponent had to guess which cylinder was in which hand. Various methods were used to baffle the guesser. The score was kept with tally sticks, and the game ended when one side had won all of them.

Dice games were also very popular. They are known to have been played in prehistoric times. However, dice did not always look like the six-sided kind we use today. In the Southwest, dice could be long sticks or bone. These were tossed into the air and the pattern they formed when they fell determined the winner.

Games of skill were played as well. One of the most well-liked and biggest gambling games was the hoop-and-pole. Like many other Indian games, its origin was believed to be sacred. In other parts of North America, this was a family event, but here it was strictly a male affair. Some

▲ While onlookers watch, these Indians of the Isleta Pueblo in New Mexico play patol, a game of chance often played with stones. This photograph was taken around 1890.

Apache groups wouldn't allow women near the playing field.

To play the game a hoop ring was needed as a target, and a pole to shoot at it. Then two opponents came on the playing field. One rolled the hoop ahead of them to a certain distance. Then both players threw their poles after it along the ground. The winner was the first player to have his pole rest in such a position that when the ring stopped rolling, it fell across the pole.

The most popular game of skill among the Hopi was kickball racing. This team relay sport took place in spring and early summer amid heavy betting. The people believed that kickball racing influenced the streams to start racing. It required barefoot runners to kick a ball in front of them for 20 miles. The Zuni had a similar game, but they kicked sticks instead of balls.

Pastimes for girls and women included games of chance as well as games of skill. Winning one such game required that the player juggle four stones as she walked until she came to a designated spot.

RAIDING AND WARFARE

Europeans considered the Apache to be the most hostile groups in the Southwest. The Apache themselves distinguished between raiding and warfare. They went on raids in order to gain material goods from the enemy, primarily livestock. Such activities were usually undertaken due to a shortage of food and raiding parties generally did not exceed 15 men from one local group. The objective was to obtain a food supply without being seen. If confronted, the warrior's goal was to make a quick escape, rather than to get caught in a bloody battle. However, if forced to fight, the Apache were well prepared for combat, having trained for such eventualities from an early age.

War parties served a different purpose than raids. They were organized to avenge Apache casualties that had been previously suffered in battle. A slain warrior's kin usually initiated the call for a war party and then played a major role in combat. A war party could consist of as many as 200 men, recruited from a number of different local groups.

Apache trained from childhood to be expert warriors. Both girls and boys were taught to be swift and strong. Although the girls were also brought up to be obedient wives and mothers, they were known to often accompany the men in raiding parties.

At times, the Apache and the Pueblo Indians were on friendly terms, and worked together to oust the Spanish. After the Pueblo became more friendly with the Spanish, the Apache no longer were friendly toward their former allies, and hostilities intensified.

The Apache relatives, the Navajo, also were raiders, which forced other tribes to guard themselves against the tribe. However, although raiding parties were formed by the Navajo, these people also spent time each year near their farming sites. When sheep were introduced to the region, the Navajo became even more sedentary.

Although the Tohono O'odham and Pima Indians were primarily peaceful people, they often had no choice but to fight to defend themselves against the Apache who regularly attacked them in the winters and stole their crops. In most Tohono O'odham and Pima villages, war parties were led by a war leader. Their weapons included bows and arrows, and wooden clubs.

Other Indian tribes in the Southwest that often engaged in hostilities were the River Yuman tribes, which were organized into strong tribal groups that waged war against their neighbors as well as fellow Yuman. The Upper Yuman Yavapai linked up with the Apache and eventually were assimilated.

TRADE

Trade has been going on for thousands of years among the Indians of the Southwest. Indians traded items that they made, grew, gathered, or had from other earlier trades. In prehistoric times, such items included the blue-green stone turquoise, today frequently found in ruins in the form of pendants. Turquoise was used in many ceremonies. It was mined in the Southwest and apparently traded as far south as Mexico.

The Pueblo were especially adept at trading. They traded among their many villages, as well as with other Indians. After the Spanish came, the newcomers fit into the trade network, and a way of life that benefitted everyone.

For instance, the Havasupai mined red ocher from deposits in their area. This produced a red

▲ San Juan, a Mescalero Apache chief, is shown here holding his spear and shield.

paint that was in demand. The Hopi, who didn't know the locations of these deposits, traded their textiles and pottery to the Havasupai for red ocher, as well as tanned buckskin. The tanned buckskin came from the Hualapai Indians, who had deer on their land.

Then the Hopi traded the red ocher to the Spaniards who had settled in New Mexico. It was used by Spanish women of Santa Fe as both a rouge for their cheeks and as a protection against the sun.

The Havasupai also traded their red ocher and tanned buckskins to the Navajo for blankets, jewelry, and horses.

LIVING ON THE LAND

◄ The way in to an underground kiva, or ceremonial chamber, was down a ladder. This kiva is part of an Anasazi structure at the Cedar Mesa complex in southeastern Utah.

▼ Navajo live today in Canyon de Chelly much as their ancestors did. The domed hogan at right is the winter home; the structure on the left is used in the summer.

▲ The giant saguaro cactus, which grows to be many times the height of a person, was important to the Southwestern Indians. They ate its fruit, and drank its fermented juices. Some tribes used its ribs to build fences and homes.

PLANTS OF IMPORTANCE

▶ The agave (also called mescal) plant was the most valuable wild food for many Southwestern people, who relied upon it for food, drinks, needles and threads, and more.

▼ Once an important food for the Southwestern Indians, the mesquite shrub produces a bean that can be pounded when dried into a sweet-tasting flour.

▲ Yucca, a valuable desert plant, serves as a food, as well as a source for fiber. The Hopi use the roots in hair washing, an important part of most Hopi ceremonies.

THE IMPORTANCE OF CORN

◀ Once the corn was dried, the ancient cliff dweller often stored it, still on the cob, in stone pits. The pits were very well built and sheltered. The well-preserved corn shown here was stored at Gila Cliff Dwellings National Monument around 1300.

▼ Indian corn comes in many colorful varieties. While some corn is quickly consumed, much of the crop is dried and later pulverized into meal.

ANIMALS OF IMPORTANCE

◀ The mule deer gets its name from its huge, mule-like ears. This animal was very important to the Native Americans. They ate its meat, used its hide for clothing and shelter, and used its bones and sinews to make tools.

▼ Prairie dogs once formed an important source of food in the Southwest, where they were shot with bow and arrow or dug out of their burrows.

▲ The pronghorn antelope was another important food
source. The beautiful skins were used to make clothing
and ceremonial garb.

CHAPTER THREE

RITUAL AND RELIGION

ndian life in the Southwest is filled with many creation stories. Each of these give the people a sense of unity with the world around them, and an explanation for where they come from and why things are the way they are today. Many of the creation myths tell of the emergence of the people of the different tribes from a home beneath their ancestral grounds.

CREATION STORIES

Although various Pueblo creation teachings differ in context, they generally share the belief that the ancient people were first led up to Earth from the underground by a war chief and his assistants, who were themselves in turn guided by the Great Spirit.

According to Joe S. Sando, a renowned Pueblo scholar, the ancient people were first led to the Four Corners area, where they settled for many hundreds of years. Then the Great Spirit ordered them to disperse by groups in many different directions. They obeyed, moving to new areas, and developing different dialects as they learned to live in harmony with nature and endure natural hardships, such as floods and droughts.

Finally, the Great Spirit led the ancient ones to a land where they would be safe. Here they were reminded of all they had suffered, and of all they had to give thanks for. They were taught how to live off this new land and how to plant and harvest the food, especially the corn. The Great Spirit also instructed the people to respect nature, as well as their leaders. The Pueblo people were told to defend themselves from future enemies by building fortress-like structures. Twin warrior gods play a prominent part in Pueblo creation stories, and the people were told to pray to them for aid in time of trouble. The Great One returned to his home far away, leaving the people in each Pueblo under the spiritual leadership of its cacique and his assistants.

In one Pueblo creation story, that of the Zuni, the two war gods, the sons of the sun, led the ancient people through four worlds before coming to the present one. After traveling very far, the war gods decided that one of them should send his children, a boy and a girl, on ahead. Their task would be to find a permanent home.

The brother and sister climbed a high mountain from which they could see the country around them, and they decided to make the mountain their home. This was Thunder Mountain, which has held a prominent place in Zuni life for centuries. It is their major shrine, with thousands of prayer sticks scattered over it.

The Hopi and other Pueblo tribes believe that they came from the underground world through a place known as a sipapu. When they die, they will return to the place of their origin. The Hopi say that their original sipapu is located deep at the bottom of the Grand Canyon.

The Navajo have many versions of their creation story. However, each begins with a journey upward to Earth through a number of subterranean worlds. In each of these worlds, the ancients try to live orderly lives, but their destructive traits, such as jealousy, quarreling, incest, and adultery force them into a pattern of failure. Eventually, each new world is destroyed, and the ancients flee to the next world through an opening in it. Every time they are saved they vow to live better lives in the new world. They always have trouble keeping their promises.

In some versions, major figures in the creation of the Navajo world come into being before the world of Earth is reached. These include First Man and First Woman, as well as the sacred medicine bundle that contains the objects and powers from which will come the Navajo world.

When First Man and First Woman reach Earth they carefully plan out what the new world will be like, then open their medicine bundle and transform the objects inside it into The Holy People. They also construct a ceremonial house (hogan) in which to create the Navajo world. Here, in the center of the house they create a mini-world that is in turn transformed into the Navajo world of today.

After the creation has been accomplished and meets the approval of dawn and evening twilight, which are two human-shaped forms, an important cultural heroine is born into this beautiful and orderly world. This is Changing Woman, whose parents are identified with the sacred objects of thought and speech in the medicine bundle.

Changing Woman has twin sons fathered by the sun: Monster Slayer and Born of the Water. She and her sons improve the new world before she creates the first Navajo people. The cosmic creation is completed with the departure of the Holy People, who return to the underworld, but promise to forever watch over and direct all aspects of Navajo life.

Apache stories have many similarities to those of the Navajo, and like the Navajo, they have a cultural heroine. To many groups, including the Chiricahua, she is known as White-Painted Woman. She and her son, Child of the Water, gave many customs to the tribe. The Mescalero also revere White-Painted Woman and Child of the Water, who they believe was miraculously conceived after White-Painted Woman allowed water to drip upon her head from an overhanging rock ledge. From the age of four, Child of the Water challenged evil monsters and eventually killed them all.

The Western Apache, who share many customs with the Navajo, also consider Changing Woman their great cultural heroine. Her son, Slayer of Monsters, was fathered by the Sun, while her son Child of the Water was the child of Black Water (one of the forces who had helped to shape the Earth). These half-brothers must fight the evil creatures on Earth before this world can become a fit place for the people.

Coyote is another important cultural figure to the Apache and many other Southwestern Indians. He is a cunning, deceitful character who at the same time brings many beneficial things to his people, although this often happens by accident. The Western Apache credit Coyote with teaching them many things, including how to plant corn and gather mescal, as well as how to weave baskets and smoke tobacco. Stories of Coyote's foolishness are used to educate children in the right ways of doing things, which are often just the opposite of how Coyote does them.

According to the Tohono O'odham and Pima, the whole world was made from dirt supplied by their supreme spiritual beings, Earthmaker and Itoi (Eetoy). Itoi is a mischievous character whose home is the underground Cave I'itoi ki, hidden at the base of the cliffs that form the walls of Baboquivari Canyon. This canyon today is part of the Tohono O'odham reservation.

Itoi and Earthmaker were unhappy with the first people in the world, so they destroyed them with a flood. But first, the two went into hiding. They made a promise that when the water receded, whoever came out of his hiding place first would be Elder Brother. Itoi earned the title. He created new people out of clay and for a long time he took care of them. But eventually he began arguing with the people and they attempted to kill him.

Itoi went under the ground to find allies in his battle against the people he had made. He found the Tohono O'odham and Pima. With their assistance, he drove away the clay people. Itoi rewarded his helpers by letting them settle on the land. He also taught them special ceremonies to bring the rain.

CEREMONIES AND RITUALS

Ceremonies are very much a part of life in the Southwest. Many involve special prayers and rituals to assure rain, because the life of every plant and animal depends so much upon the rainfall. Each tribal group brings its own spiritual beliefs to the ceremonies, which constantly keep these Native Americans in touch with the spiritual world. Many ceremonies were held to mark various events in a person's life.

Marriage was a major event in the lives of most of the Southwestern Indian tribes. In some tribes, such as the Havasupai, marriage required little more than the couple moving into a house that the new husband built for them. In other tribes, much elaborate ritual and tradition went into the union of a man and a woman.

Even today, among the traditional Hopi, the only way for a man to court a woman he cares about is to visit her while she is grinding corn at night. If she does not care for him, she continues her task. But when the right one comes along,

▲ This lightweight, easily handled cradleboard provided a safe way to transport an Apache infant.

she stops her grinding and speaks to him. If her family also approves of her choice, a wedding is in the making.

Hopi weddings can take years of preparation. Many gifts are exchanged and many ceremonies are performed before the wedding takes place. The woman and her family have special prenuptial duties. The bride-to-be must stay with the man's parents for three days, while she is tested for her cooking skills, as well as her temperament and manner.

Her family makes a special basket for the groom, while the groom's male relatives weave the fabric for the bride's ceremonial cotton gown. She wears her wedding gown for the final time in death at her burial, when the Hopi be-

▲ An Apache bride in her wedding outfit.

▲ A Navajo baby on a cradleboard sees a lamb approaching. When Navajo children are old enough to share in the tasks of caring for the herd—around the age of five—they are given lambs of their own to tend.

lieve that they enter the other world through the opening known as Maski, at the bottom of the Grand Canyon.

In the past, an Apache man had a different way of showing his interest in a woman. He traditionally left meat he had hunted outside her parents' wickiup. If the woman's family approved of him, the meat was taken inside. If not, it was returned to the man, who knew he had to take his affections elsewhere.

Although traditions vary, Native Americans in the Southwest had a variety of special ceremonies to welcome a child into the world.

When a Pueblo woman gave birth, her mother was in charge. The new grandmother had to purify the infant with a sacred bath of yucca suds. The Pueblo along the Rio Grande generally believe that the spirit of a baby doesn't arrive until four days after birth. Before that time a baby has no name. Then, a ritual is performed. Two pine boughs are offered in six directions with a prayer that the infant's life be one that brightens the lives of others. As the baby is named, cornmeal— which is considered sacred in such ceremonies— is sprinkled at the doorway of the home.

Among the Hopi, when a woman has a child, mother and baby are cared for by the new grandmother and an aunt for 20 days. They all retreat to a darkened room away from the rest of the people; the baby is presented to the sun in a naming ceremony. The baby is fed corn mush, since corn is the sacred food of the Hopi.

In times past, a Tohono O'odham mother and her new baby would stay in a special house for a month after the birth. Then a sunrise ceremony was held, at which the medicine man gave the baby a name that had come to him in a dream. This name was never spoken. Instead, nicknames were used.

Among many of the tribes, when boys and girls reached puberty, around 12 to 14 years old, they had special ceremonies. Girls often went through rituals, while boys had tests of their strength and skills.

As Apache children grew up, they were given the same training in raiding and fighting skills. Both boys and girls practiced daily with bows and arrows. However, at puberty the boys generally had endurance tests, while the girls experienced extensive rites that did not involve tests of physical stamina. The Sunrise Dance, held for Apache girls who have begun to menstruate, is the most well-known puberty rite in the area. It is still performed.

Among the Navajo, both girls and boys receive their initiation into the rituals of Navajo religion during the eighth day of the nine-day Night Chant ceremony. At this time, boys are blessed with sacred meal and then ceremonially whipped with yucca leaves by a masked Yeibichai. The Yeibichais are people dressed to represent powerful spiritual beings. The girls are touched with cornmeal on various parts of their bodies, then their ears are marked with ears of corn wrapped in spruce twigs.

Afterwards, the Yeibichais remove their masks so that the children learn that the spiritual figures are really human beings just like them.

Among the Tohono O'odham, boys are expected to make long runs across the desert until they become exhausted and the vision of an animal comes to them. Each boy is taught the magic powers given to him by the animal he sees. Tohono O'odham girls are not expected to have visions.

However, the coming of age of Tohono O'odham girls has its own rituals. As in many Native American tribes, menstruation among the Tohono O'odham was considered a great mys-

▲ Dressed as a Yeibichai, or powerful spiritual being, this Navajo medicine man wears a mask over his face. After he participates in a ceremony, he will remove the mask to show that he is really just a human being.

tery. Each Tohono O'odham family unit had a separate house where the women stayed once a month, during her menstrual cycle. This house was set up away from the others and faced the opposite direction, because the Tohono O'odham believed that a woman had magical powers at this time of month and could endanger the men if she remained in their presence.

Death was another great mystery to the Southwestern Indians. Most tribes either buried or cremated their dead.

The Pueblo buried their dead in traditional attire, and included in the grave food, drink, and tools that could be of use to them in the next world. They did this as soon as possible after the death had taken place. Then they watched the burial place for four days. By then they believed that the spirit of the deceased was safely in the spirit realm.

The Apache avoided burial grounds, however. They never spoke the name of the dead and they burned the property of the deceased. They even changed the names of children who had been frequently mentioned by the deceased. The Navajo also had a strong fear of the dead, and were quick to burn everything belonging to them.

The Havasupai also burned the property of the dead, as did the Pima. The Pima cut their hair when in mourning over the death of a close relative and buried it in the sand of a riverbed. Pima widows were expected to mourn for four years, during which time they couldn't wash their hair.

Like most other Southwestern tribes, the Pueblo Indians frequently use symbols in their ceremonies and rituals. Every song, gesture, action, article of clothing, and ritual object has a symbolic meaning. The sun, the moon, the wind, the rain, and other elements of nature are critical to the Pueblo and meant to be honored.

All ceremonies in most of the Pueblo villages take place both in the kivas, or underground chambers, and in the plazas. Every kiva has a group of dancers who perform at least once in every kiva in the village. If a dance has female roles, the men and boys take the roles of women.

Before planting, and at harvest time, the Pueblo perform sacred rites. They undertake the same before going on hunts. Many such rites are led by the sacred leaders who spend much time in ritual fasting and prayer.

However, the most important ceremonies are performed by special societies that have their own priests, altars, sacred symbols, and objects.

These groups are usually only open to men. When a boy comes of age in his early teens, he can be initiated into one of the societies. Then he will be told his society's ancient stories. He will also learn how to pray properly and perform the sacred ceremonies.

The participants in some ceremonies wear regalia that have been passed down from one generation to another. It is a great honor and responsibility to wear them.

While much of the sacred religious life of the Pueblo takes place within the kivas, important ceremonies are performed in the central plaza of a pueblo. Before a ceremony, the men must purify themselves. They wash their hair in yucca leaf suds and drink a mixture that makes them throw up to clean out their insides.

Pueblo religious life includes prayer sticks. These are usually carved out of wood and have feathers attached. Prayers are often accompanied by the placing of prayer sticks at sacred shrines, as well as at natural places that are believed to be spiritually powerful. The sticks are intended to attract the attention of the spirits.

The Kachinas are a major group of spirit rainmakers to many of the Pueblo, especially the Hopi and Zuni. The Kachinas are masked figures that both bring rain and general well-being. Some Kachinas are said to live in the mountains and waters; others dwell in the clouds and under the ground. According to tradition, the Kachinas came to the Pueblo villages long ago when the people needed help. They danced and caused the rains to fall so that the crops would grow. They also gave the people gifts and taught them skills in hunting and in crafts. Their presence brought harmony to the universe.

Then one day the Kachinas and the people got involved in a dispute. As a result, the Kachinas left, refusing to return. However, they agreed that the people could wear ceremonial masks and regalia and impersonate Kachinas.

Today, the Hopi count over 250 different Kachinas. However, the number changes annually, because old Kachinas are discarded, and new ones are added each year.

Kachina masked dances are performed in the pueblos during the first six months of the year,

RAIN DANCES

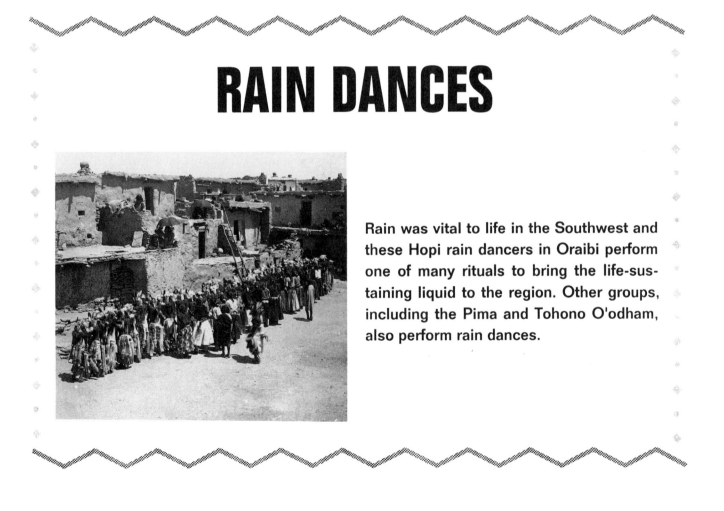

Rain was vital to life in the Southwest and these Hopi rain dancers in Oraibi perform one of many rituals to bring the life-sustaining liquid to the region. Other groups, including the Pima and Tohono O'odham, also perform rain dances.

▲ In this 1903 photo, taken at the Hopi Second Mesa village of Shonghopavi, Arizona, masked Kachinas are performing one of many dances to bring rain.

beginning with the arrival of the spirit beings in the Hopi villages following the winter solstice. At such times, the children receive gifts, including rattles, moccasins, and dolls dressed to represent the various Kachinas. However, these dolls aren't meant to be played with. They are for teaching the children about the virtues possessed by each Kachina.

Before the Kachinas return to their spiritual homes each year, they visit the Hopi for the last time in a ceremony held in July. They dance at night, then disappear, except for a few of the most important who appear the next morning to ceremonially close the kivas to Kachinas for another year.

Another important Hopi Kachina dance takes place in February. This is the Powamu (Bean Dance), at which Kachinas bring samples of the new bean sprouts. This seems magical to the children, since the ground is covered with snow at this time of year. (The beans have actually been grown inside the kivas.)

The chief Kachina is known as Eototo. He controls the seasons and is the main performer in the Bean Dance. Eototo wears white, except for his red moccasins and a trace of blue over one shoulder. He carries a small wand in one hand and a gourd with sacred water in the other. Attoli, with his wand or staff, appears with Eototo in the Bean Dance. He is the Chief's Lieutenant,

and wears a high mask that is cone-shaped and often painted with many colors.

The Koyemsi, or mudhead clowns, appear at all Hopi Kachina dances. The Koyemsi clown around in between dances of other Kachinas. The mudhead have masks and bodies painted a reddish brown. They wear kilts and each carries a rattle and a feather. The Zuni also have clowns; they are known as Koyemsi.

Today, the most important ceremony given by the Apache is the girls' puberty rite. The Western Apache call it the Sunrise Ceremony. It is their most elaborate ritual.

Preparing for the dance takes as long as a year. The dance itself lasts for four days and four nights. The ceremony also involves the building of a sacred tipi, which will be taken down at its end. The tipi represents the universe.

There are both solemn private rituals and public activities, including feasting, as part of the Sunrise Ceremony. During the ritual two people are especially important to the young girl. One of them is an older woman, who leads the girl through the ritual and remains close to her throughout the rest of their lives. The other person is a male. He is the singer, whose songs are meant to guide the young girl to live a long and healthy life.

During the Sunrise Ceremony, the girl herself is identified with White-Painted Woman, mother of all Apache people, and wears a costume that is a copy of that worn by her. She also is addressed as White Painted Woman and is thought to have special powers at this time.

Each night male dancers perform around a bonfire. The dancers are dressed as the Mountain Spirits who live in caves. Their bodies are painted and black masks cover their faces. On their heads they wear intricate cottonwood sticks that are painted and decorated with feathers. The festivities end with all-night singing, followed by the singer painting himself and the girl. Additional ritual is performed, including a walk by the girl on a path marked with holy pollen on an animal skin, so that she may live a long and happy life.

When the ceremony is finished, the girl and her female attendant separate from the group for a four-day retreat. When the girl returns to her parent's dwelling, she is eligible to get married.

Virtually every action in Navajo life has a rite to accompany it, either for protection or for healing purposes. Many rituals are based on ancient stories and both take the form of chants that re-

▲ Masked Mud Heads, or Koyemsi, prepare to dance for spectators seated on the upper walls of the Zuni Pueblo. This photo was taken in 1879.

late the story and apply to the ceremony being performed.

The most frequently observed ceremony is the Blessing Way. The chant for this occasion reenacts the ancient time at which mortals were created and taught how to live in harmony with this world. The Blessing Way chant is sung throughout each Navajo's life, beginning before a child is about born.

Blessing Way is meant to protect the person and his or her family and provide them with increased prosperity. There are five kinds of Blessing Way rituals, and these are used, not only for childbirth, but also for blessing a new hogan, installing tribal officers, making ceremonial paraphernalia holy, protecting livestock as well as warriors, and more.

The ritual itself is relatively brief, lasting two nights. The only essential equipment for performing this rite is the mountain soil bundle. This is a buckskin bundle with small amounts of soil that come from the sacred mountains, as well as certain stone objects and prayer sticks. Pollen (usually from corn) is used and personifies Corn Pollen Boy and Corn Beetle Girl, who are Navajo symbols of fertility, happiness, and life. Pollen is applied to everything from the person receiving the blessing to the spectators, ritual objects, and hogan to sanctify all.

The Yaqui have many traditional ceremonies with much pageantry that deal with the battle between Good and Evil. When the Spaniards brought Christianity to the area, many tribes resisted the new religion. However, the Yaqui

found that the story of Christ fitted in well with their own religious concepts. Today, they are noted for their Easter Week dramas, which can be seen in Arizona's Yaqui villages.

MEDICINE

Medicine people were very important throughout the Indian communities of the American Southwest. They were called upon to cure both physical and mental ailments. Some tribes, such as the Apache, had many different medicine people, each with the ability to cure a different problem. Others had more general practitioners.

Medicine people were also expected to conduct major ceremonies, including life-cycle events such as births and deaths and to influence raids, hunts, and sports so that their outcomes would be positive. Most medicine people were men, although women were also known to perform curing ceremonies in some tribes, including the Mohave, Yuma, Apache, and Navajo.

Most Indians of the Southwest believe that illness strikes when an alien object enters the body. This is most often caused by someone breaking a tribal taboo or by witchcraft. Each tribe had its own taboos. The Hopi considered animal abuse to be a serious taboo, and the Apache considered it dangerous to see or even walk in the tracks of certain animals, including the owl, snake, and coyote.

When illness struck, a medicine person was summoned to restore harmony to the patient by removing the foreign substance from the victim's body. Often this took the form of the sucking cure, in which the medicine person appears to suck the invading object out of the victim. The "appearance" is not meant to fool the patient, but to encourage the person to feel that he or she is being healed.

In many tribes, novice medicine people were apprenticed for many years to practicing medicine men or women who were paid large sums for their services. Some initiates were chosen because they showed traits that revealed their "medicine power." Others inherited the position from blood relatives. Yuman medicine people most often received their healing powers through dreams.

Navajo medicine people are still highly regarded in their tribes. Navajo apprentices can be as young as six years old, if they show the traits that make a good medicine person: including discipline, excellent memory, and curiosity.

▲ A Navajo medicine man, in a picture taken in 1914.
Today many Native Americans consult both medical doctors and medicine men when they are ill.

▲ This 1927 photo shows Pueblo women making pottery outside an adobe house in the Tewa-speaking San Ildefonso Pueblo, New Mexico.

Among the Navajo, medicine people are considered singers because they use complex chants in their cures. They must make sure to sing the chants exactly right if the cure is to work and not harm the patient. For this reason, Navajo medicine men (some women are also singers, but they are very few) are not expected to memorize more than four ceremonies in a whole lifetime.

Navajo medicine men also use sand paintings (also known as dry paintings) in many of their healing ceremonies. Sand paintings are also made by Tohono O'odham, Apache, and Pueblo medicine people. However, the Navajo sand paintings are the most widely known. They were often made from colored sandstone, as well as from pulverized flowers, and were symbolic pictures often with one or more heros or heroines of an ancient story, or the Holy People represented in their complexity. Navajo healing ceremonies with their sand paintings are still very much in use today. The sand painter and singer begins creating the ceremony's sand painting early in the morning. However, no matter how long it takes to complete, it will be destroyed at sunset.

But each Navajo healing ceremony requires more than sand paintings and chants. These intricate rituals also involve appropriate purification fasts and baths, chants, sacred objects, holy pollen, medicines, singers, and much more.

A variety of such ceremonies exists; one of the longest ceremonies is the Night Chant, which takes nine days. There are two versions of this chant: one has a sand painting for each of the nine days, the other does not. There is so much to learn before being able to perform this cor-

▲ Santa Clara, a Tewa-speaking pueblo, is known for the magnificent pottery made by the residents. The pueblo is named for St. Clare, a nun of the13th century.

▲ Nampeyo, a master Pueblo pottery maker, with examples of her work. By duplicating the pottery forms and designs of her ancestors, Nampeyo helped bring Hopi pottery to new levels of distinction.

rectly, the singer of the Night Chant may not be ready to perform the ceremony in public until he is in his forties.

The sand painter begins at sunrise in the special ceremonial hogan. He draws from memory, with colors from the earth: red and brown from sandstone, yellow from crushed corn, black from wood charcoal, and white from limestone.

The patient is not permitted to view the painting until it is completed. Then he or she is invited into the hogan and seated in the center of the painting, facing east. The healing ceremony continues, with the medicine man chanting while shaking his rattle. Sand is applied from the painting to the patient, cigarettes are smoked, herbal drinks are served, and holy pollen is strewn on the painting.

In all Navajo ceremonies, pollen is the most important medicine. The pollen of the cattail was once most often used and is still regarded as the only "real" pollen, but now corn pollen frequently replaces it. Pollen—symbol of fertility, safety, and long life—is supposed to bring the blessings of peace, happiness, and prosperity.

At the end of the day, after the medicine man completely destroys his painting, the colored sands are scattered to the north outside of the hogan, and become part of the earth once again.

The Apache have many ceremonies to cure illnesses. These are led by a medicine person, who achieves power through visions, during which he or she is taught the appropriate healing songs and receives the objects needed to attract spiritual help in curing rituals. Sacred substances include pollen, white shell, and turquoise. Female shamans were common among the Apache, especially among the Chiricahua and Mescalero. They often specialized in the use of herb cures.

Among Pueblo, small, secret medicine societies initiate members into their powers. In many pueblos, they deal only with sickness that comes from spiritual causes. They may also manage the ceremonies that take place throughout the year.

The Piman curing ceremony is performed by lay people, rather than by a medicine person, and involves blowing and singing as important ritual acts. The songs for both Piman and Tohono O'odham curing ceremonies must be carefully learned, since only the proper song petitions the spirit to effect a cure. The healer asks for help on behalf of the patient, rather than curing the patient himself.

MEDICINAL PLANTS

Although much of the knowledge has been lost, many American Indians in the Southwest knew about the medicinal power of their local plants, and such knowledge is still used or being revived today. Some medicinal plants were only used by certain tribes, others were known far and wide.

Many tribes knew how to split the pads of prickly pear cactus and soak them as a poultice (a kind of moist pad) to help heal wounds. The Hopi and the Apache used the pitch of various pinon pines on cuts and sores. They also boiled mesquite gum to make a wash for cuts, and they used mesquite sap for eye problems by applying it directly to the troubled eye.

The Hopi crushed the roots of cattail and mixed it with fat as a salve for burns, while the Zuni made a poultice for burns by mixing a crushed yarrow plant with water.

The Pima made an elderberry flower tea for colds, fevers, and sore throats. They treated stomachache and diarrhea with a tea made from the leaves of creosote bush or from mesquite leaves. The Pima also made a mesquite tea for headache and considered mesquite a general tonic for the whole body.

To keep away insects, Indians of the Southwest rubbed onions on their skin. If an insect did bite, the pain was eased with a poultice made

▲ Three Hopi women are busy weaving baskets in the village of Shipaulovi.

from the crushed leaves of Rocky Mountain bee-weed. Sweatbaths were used to cure many illnesses and to purify the body before ceremonies. The Apache also used them to aid their running abilities. These baths were taken in sweatlodges, often low, windowless structures, in which medicinal plants were added to water that was poured over heated rocks.

Today, Indians of the Southwest consult their traditional medicine people for help when they are sick. Contemporary Indians often use modern medical practitioners, too. A combination of traditional and contemporary doctors works best

▲ Navajo women expanded the art of weaving and developed it into an industry for the Dene, as the Navajo call themselves. Here, a Navajo woman spins wool into yarn to weave on the loom behind her.

▲ Among the Hopi, weaving was a man's work and he supplied all the clothing his family needed.

for them. The modern practitioner usually treats only the patient's body, while the traditional medicine person heals the spirit, as well.

SOUTHWEST INDIAN ARTS

The Southwestern Indians are outstanding artists with a tradition that goes back many centuries, to prehistoric rock paintings found on canyon walls. Works of art by Southwestern artists and artisans are in great demand throughout the world, as new craftspeople are bringing the skills of their ancestors to a new level of beauty for all to enjoy.

Southwestern Indian potters are generally women. They have been making pottery for centuries. Pottery was first produced in this area by the ancestors of today's tribes, who lived here about 1,600 years ago. The Hohokam, ancestors of the Tohono O'odham, are also known to have created pottery.

Pottery was made with clay that was found at clay beds, in the form of slabs and chunks. These had to be pounded and ground up until they were very fine. Then they were mixed with some kind of tempering so that the pottery would not crack when drying. Tempering could be fine sand, powdered shells, or crushed soapstone.

Smaller pots could be pressed into shape with the fingers, while larger ones were built up in coils. The only tools used were a variety of gourd pieces, pebbles, and sticks.

When a pot was finished, it was first dried, then scraped on the outside with pieces of broken pottery or gourd shell to smooth the sides. A thin mixture of clay and water known as slip was applied with a rabbit's tail. Some pots were given several coats of slip. This created a background upon which a design could be painted.

The potter painted her designs with brushes made from the stems of the yucca plant. After the paint dried, the pot was fired. A fire was built and allowed to burn to coals. Then a platform of stone was placed across the coals, and the pot set upside down upon it.

The pottery of the Pueblo villages exhibits many distinctive styles. Acoma Pueblo is known for its thin-walled and light pottery, while Zuni designs are distinguished by their simplicity and abstractions. The pueblos of San Ildefonso and Santa Clara are famous for their unusual, highly polished black and red pottery.

Basketweaving is one of the most ancient crafts in the Southwest. Early weavers used different grasses, roots, and stems to produce bowls and jars, as well as pots and carrying vessels.

▲ Although Apache women made little pottery, they excelled in basketwork. This collection, photographed in 1893, belonged to a United States Army lieutenant in the 11th Infantry.

▲ A Navajo silversmith displays examples of his tools and work, including a concha belt, made in the shape of shells. Navajo silversmiths learned their craft in the late 1800s from the Mexicans. This picture was taken around 1880, so the silversmith shown here is an early practitioner of the art.

When woven baskets were intended to carry liquid, they were made watertight with a covering of pitch from the pinon pine.

Woven burden baskets were made throughout the Southwest, though the Apache are most famous for making them. Burden baskets are containers for small objects that women carry on their backs. The Apache baskets were made most often from willow, cottonwood, or mulberry, and fringed with buckskin. The Pima and Tohono O'odham made their burden baskets out of a net of twine supported on a frame of poles.

The Navajo are the most well-known of the Southwestern Indian weavers. However, their weaving is fairly recent. They appear to have first acquired this art from the Pueblo Indians sometime during the early 19th century.

Men are the weavers among the Pueblo. They were weaving cotton long before the Spanish arrived. After the Spaniards introduced herds of sheep, weaving with wool became widespread.

Among the Navajo, the women control the weaving industry. They do all their work by hand, including carding or combing the wool, spinning the thread, and preparing the dyes. Then they weave their rugs on upright looms.

At first, the Navajo only wove blankets for clothing. Now their colorful designs are used for both wall hangings and rugs and are in great demand by collectors around the world.

The designs that Navajo women weave on their rugs are passed on from mother to daughter. The earliest designs used were simple shapes, such as stripes, zigzags, and diamonds. Later, figures were added, including spiritual beings. Some designs came from sand paintings.

Originally, the Navajo had only three natural colors to choose from, a rusty black, white, and a brownish gray. Today, colors come from many sources, and there are over 250 recipes for making vegetable dyes. These include pink from potato peelings, and olive green from mistletoe.

People often think of the Navajo as ancient silversmiths. However, they did not learn the craft until the late 1850s. At that time they traded their horses to Mexican silversmiths for silver ornaments. The Navajo were strongly influenced by Mexican designs, many of which originated in Spain. There is a Spanish flavor to Navajo silver buttons, hollow beads, and squash blossom necklaces. The blossom was inspired by an ornament on the seams of trousers worn by Spaniards.

The Navajo got other ideas for designs from the silver jewelry they obtained in trade from the Plains Indians. These include concha belts, which the Navajo fashioned after those worn by enemy tribesmen on the Great Plains. The word *concha* is from the Spanish word meaning shell.

The Zuni learned silversmithing from the Navajo. They began adding turquoise to their silver bracelets, pins, and rings before the turn of the century, at which time the stone first became widely used.

In this century, the Hopi developed overlay, a new style in silverwear, based on their pottery patterns. Two pieces of silver are combined with the top piece etched out. The craftsmanship is so fine that the finished article appears to be a single piece.

Contemporary Southwestern pottery, basketry, weavings, and jewelry are in demand by people who value the skill, as well as the spirit, that goes into making them.

Indian artists of the Southwest are making their mark on painting, sculpture, and music, as well. R. Carlos Nakai is one of today's most respected Southwest Indian musicians. Part Navajo and part Ute, Nakai has made many records playing his personal and beautiful sounds on a Native American wooden flute. He tells aspiring musicians that the instrument is closely linked to tribal vocal music and cannot be played unless one can sing tribal melodies and understand tribal lifeways.

▶ A Pueblo man plays his wooden flute in a photograph taken around 1890. Traditionally, a man courted a woman by playing the flute to her. Flutes were also used in healing ceremonies.

RITUAL AND ART

▶ Kachinas, or spirit rainmakers, are important figures in Hopi and Zuni belief. Dolls dressed to represent the Kachinas are given to children, but they are not toys. Instead, they are used to teach the children about the Kachinas. There are about 250 different Kachinas; this Hopi Kachina represents the Black Ogre.

▼ Elaborate paintings made of colored sand, ground minerals, and pollen are made by Navajo medicine men for healing ceremonies. The paintings can take many hours to produce, but they are always destroyed at the end of the day. To photograph one would mean that an image of the painting still exists, and so no cameras are allowed when a sand painting is made. However, sometimes watercolor paintings that show the design of the sand paintings are made. This photograph shows a watercolor copy of a sand painting of the Thunder Gods, used in the Navajo Shooting Chant.

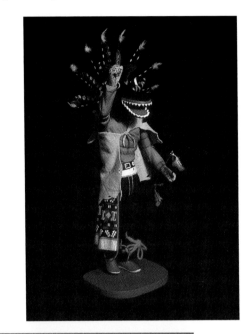

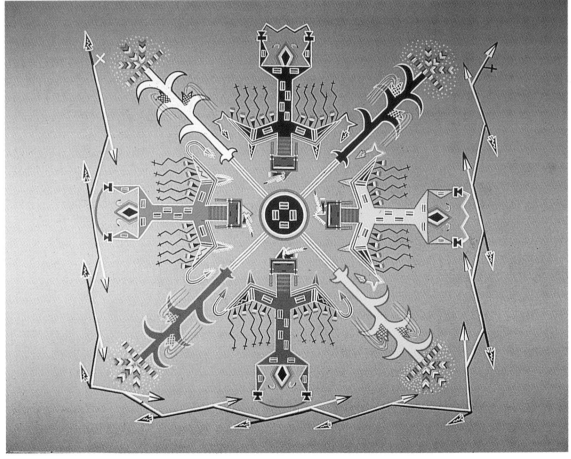

CEREMONIAL STRUCTURES

◀ At Bandelier National Monument, near Sante Fe, New Mexico, cliff dwellings and cave dwellings, including reconstructed kivas, can be visited today.

▼ The sweat lodge was an important part of Navajo life. To take a purifying sweat bath, the men would crowd inside, close the door, and pour water over hot rocks to make steam (much like a sauna).

ROCK ART

◀ These rock carvings, or petroglyphs, on soft sandstone walls tell stories from the past in the Southwest.

▼ This rock painting at Standing Cow Ruins in Canyon de Chelly Navajo Nation probably represents a priest or a Spanish procession. The horse, first brought to the Americas by the Spanish, would greatly change the Indian life-style.

CRAFTS THEN AND NOW

◀ Artist Ramona Sakiestewa gives a contemporary twist to traditional Hopi weaving with this wool tapestry wall hanging, titled "Star Maker."

▼ Baskets had many uses in Native American culture. This basket was made by a Pima woman around 1900.

▲ Traditional Hopi pottery is the basis for this stoneware sculpture, called "Bird Woman," by artist Otellie Loloma.

◀ The Mimbres people thrived in the Southwest from about 300 B.C. to A.D. 1300. The painted black-on-white pottery from Mimbres has more delicate designs and more masterful shaping than that found in any other ancient Southwestern pottery. The Mimbres are also known for their lively naturalistic drawings, including those of human beings and other animals. The Mimbres are believed to be descended from the Mogollon people, as were the Zuni. The Mimbres disappeared suddenly around A.D. 1300, leaving behind many pieces of pottery that were deliberately broken. No one has ever explained the mystery.

▼ After Navajo silversmiths learned the art of jewelry-making from Mexicans in the mid-1800s, they raised it to a new level, as this beautiful silver belt shows.

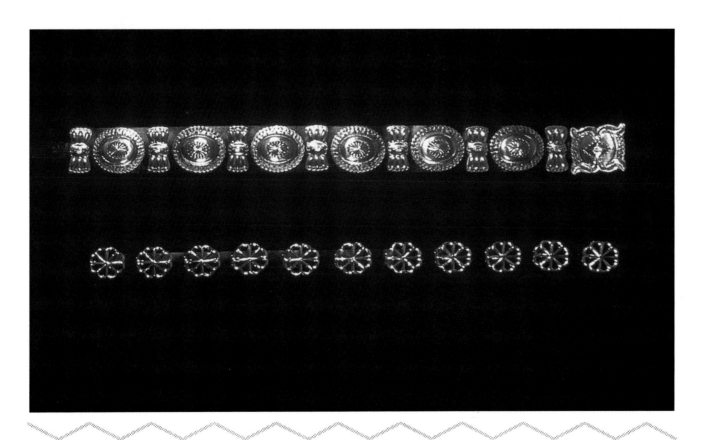

▲ The Navajo are famous for their colorful and beautiful hand-woven rugs. In 1988 the U.S. Postal Service honored their work with these postage stamps.

CHAPTER FOUR

CHANGES

he Southwestern Indians had the region to themselves until the mid-1500s. Then Spanish explorers began to arrive and the Native Americans were forced to react to the new invaders. By the time the Spanish explorer Francisco Coronado led the first non-Indians to enter a Pueblo village in 1540, the Pueblo settlements were mostly scattered along the Rio Grande and its branches. Only the Hopi and Zuni were still living near the desert homes of their original ancestors.

Coronado, along with several hundred men, had come northward from Mexico, seeking the fabled Seven Cities of Cibola. These "cities" were reportedly paved with gold. (Very likely this golden hue was caused by the sun's reflections on the land and the pueblos.) The tale of Cibola's riches had been spread by an earlier Spanish explorer, Fray Marcos de Niza, whose scouting party had been forced back by the Pueblo Indians the previous year.

This time the Spaniards with their firearms and steel swords easily captured the Zuni villages they entered. The Zuni ran from their homes to their sacred Thunder Mountain, where they sought refuge.

Much to Coronado's dismay, instead of gold-paved streets he found pueblos filled with hard-working, but poor, people. He stayed, just the same. Eventually, he thoroughly explored the Pueblo country, and reported on 66 villages.

Coronado's men also became the first Europeans to reach the Grand Canyon and to travel up the Rio Grande Valley. However, he considered his expedition a failure, since he found no fabulous treasures and no precious stones, except for turquoise.

The Spanish left the area to pursue other frontiers where rich silver deposits and new cattle ranges were found. But they were to return eventually, this time to stay.

Some 50 years after Coronado's explorations, the Spaniards began coming back to the Southwest. In 1598, Juan de Onate led an expedition into New Mexico that included soldiers, as well as hundreds of men and women settlers. They brought thousands of heads of cattle with them, as well as other animals.

The coming of the Spanish was both good and bad for the Indians. The people were taxed and sometimes enslaved. But they benefited by the introduction of new animals, such as horses, donkeys, cattle, and sheep. They tasted new foods, including wheat, green peppers, and peaches, and they learned about new tools made out of iron.

▲ Apache scouts stationed at Fort Wingate, New Mexico, are shown drilling with rifles. Many Indians, particularly Apache, served in the U.S. Army in the late 1800s.

The Spaniards also brought Christianity with them. When they built churches and insisted on converting the Indians, many villages resisted.

As Spanish rule grew more and more ruthless, the Pueblo people began uniting against the common enemy. This was not easy, since the Pueblo were spread out over an area of 300 miles.

However, a medicine man named Pope from San Juan Pueblo managed to plan a revolt in secret. He handed out knotted cords to each village chief and told them to untie one knot each day. When the last knot was untied, the uprising would begin.

Starting on August 10, 1680, the Pueblo Revolt swept through the region. In just a few days, a quarter of all the Spaniards in New Mexico were killed. Most of their churches were burned.

Following the revolt, the Indians, fearful of retaliation, deserted the less easily defensible pueblos. They headed northward, which brought them in contact with the Navajo. In some regions, the two people merged, and the Pueblo culture was adapted by the Navajo.

In 1692, a Spanish army, under the command of Don Diego de Vargas, entered the Southwest. While some Spanish historians consider De Varga compassionate toward the Pueblo, Pueblo scholars report that his methods of pacifying the people were brutal. Pueblo in support of Spain were pitted against Pueblo that were against Spanish rule.

As time went on, one pueblo after another was able to combine its familiar religion with Christianity. Tensions in the area diminished as the Pueblo returned to their old ways. Meanwhile, the Spanish busied themselves settling the new cities of Santa Fe and Albuquerque.

In 1821 when Spain granted Mexico its independence, the Pueblo country became a Mexican province. Then, in 1848, after Mexico's war with the United States, what are today New Mexico and Arizona became part of the United States.

The Pueblo Indians were considered more peaceful than the Apache and Navajo, who raided their flocks and fields. The United States government helped arm the Pueblo against their enemies. The United States authorities recognized each Pueblo village as an independent unit of local government, with full rights to the land and to self-government.

The new settlers from the East were not as

▲ Mangas Coloradas (c. 1797–1863) was a Mimbreno
Apache leader who led many raids against settlers in his
homeland in the southwestern part of New Mexico.
Mangas Coloradas was captured by trickery and killed
by American soldiers. Two famous leaders, Cochise and
Geronimo, fought under Mangas Coloradas.

▲ Apache prisoners at Fort Bowie in Arizona, around 1884. Many Apache died in captivity, the result of poor treatment and diseases to which they had no resistance.

GERONIMO (1829-1909)

Geronimo, the most famous war chief of the Chiricahua Apache, lost his mother, wife, and children in a Mexican raid. This tragedy caused him great bitterness. After serving under two great Apache leaders, Cochise and Mangas Coloradas, Geronimo led warring parties into Mexico. When non-Indians entered Apache land, Geronimo raided their settlements as well.

In 1883, upon the urging of a United States general, Geronimo moved his people to the San Carlos Reservation. However, Geronimo could not adjust to reservation life. Two years later he and his band fled south to Mexico and began their raids once more. Although he was pursued, Geronimo did not surrender until 1887.

He was sent to Fort Marion, Florida, on a train with 340 other Apache prisoners. Nearly a third died in the intense heat during their trip. In 1894, Geronimo was sent to Fort Sill, Oklahoma. He died of natural causes in 1909 without ever seeing his homeland again.

▲ Geronimo (1829–1909), a Chiricahua Apache by marriage, fought alongside Chief Cochise against the U.S. Army and became the most feared of the Apache warriors. This picture was taken in 1887.

▲ Chiricahua Apache prisoners, including Geronimo (first row, second from right), seated outside their railroad car in Arizona, about to be taken to imprisonment in a Florida camp, where they would suffer humiliation and contract disease.

generous towards the Pueblo as the government. Some ruthlessly pushed the Pueblo off pasture land that had been theirs for centuries. The Pueblo also had to worry about non-Indian gold hunters and trappers, as well as cattlemen and land speculators.

Reservations are lands held in trust by the United States for various tribes. Since the Pueblo Indians did not live on reservations they had no legal rights to their land. Instead, they had to learn how to fight in the courts for their lands against those who intruded upon them.

In 1922 the Pueblo Indians were united for the first time since the Pueblo Revolt of 1680 when they formed an organization that successfully defeated a bill that would have given non-Indian squatters the right to claim Pueblo lands. By an act of Congress, the Pueblo Lands Act went into effect in 1924. This gave back to the Pueblo some of their lost lands. It also provided some compensation for lands that could no longer be recovered.

The first meeting between the Apache and the Spanish appears to have taken place in 1541, when Coronado met a group of Apache in what is now the Texas Panhandle. These were the Querecho, who were on friendly terms with the Pueblo. They traded buffalo hides and buckskins for corn, beans, squash, and cotton cloth.

At first, there seems to have been some trading between the Apache and the Spanish. However, it wasn't long before the two became hostile to each other.

After the Spaniards settled along the Rio Grande, bands of Apache began raiding them to get their horses. Then Apache on horseback intensified their raids on other Indian tribes, as well. Their reputation as fighters grew during the 1600s as they expanded their territory, acquiring

▲ In 1882 the Apache leader Geronimo and his followers left the San Juan Reservation and began raiding white settlements. General George Crook was sent to stop him. It took Crook four years to catch Geronimo, and when he did, Geronimo escaped. In this picture, Geronimo is third from the left, wearing a bandanna on his head; Crook is second from the right.

greater hunting ranges and more fields.

Opinions about these warriors vary. Some claim that they were ferocious fighters who saw raiding as a way of life. Others blame their hostile acts on the Spaniards, who created friction between the Apache and the Pueblo with whom they traded as a tactic to divide and conquer the tribes. If this was the case, the ruse worked, for before long the Apache were both feared and hunted by other Indians.

The Spanish joined forces with Indian tribes to attack the Apache and to defend themselves against attack by them. In some cases, members of one Apache band were enlisted to fight another. Although the Apache had many great warriors, including Cochise, Geronimo, and Mangas Coloradas, such tactics eventually proved successful for the Apache foes. By the end of the 1800s most of the Apache had been moved to the reservations on which they still live.

In 1871 the White Mountain Reservation was set up for the Western Apache in eastern Arizona. In 1897 it was divided into the San Carlos and Fort Apache Reservations where Western Apache primarily live today. Some Western Apache also live on Arizona's Camp Verde Reservation, along with the Yavapai.

The Mescalero received a reservation in New Mexico in 1873, after escaping from Fort Sumner and remaining fugitives for seven years. In 1887, the Jicarilla were settled on a reservation in northwestern New Mexico.

The Chiricahua, who once lived in southeastern Arizona, southwestern New Mexico, and northern Mexico, were exiled to Florida, then to

▲ Manuelito (c. 1818–1893), a Navajo chief, played an important role in the Navajo attempt to keep white settlers from overrunning their lands.

▲ Kit Carson had an adventurous life as a trapper, scout, and military officer in the Southwest. In 1864, he led an assault on the Navajo living in Canyon de Chelly, their ancestral homeland. Carson destroyed their food supply and livestock and forced thousands of Navajo to surrender.

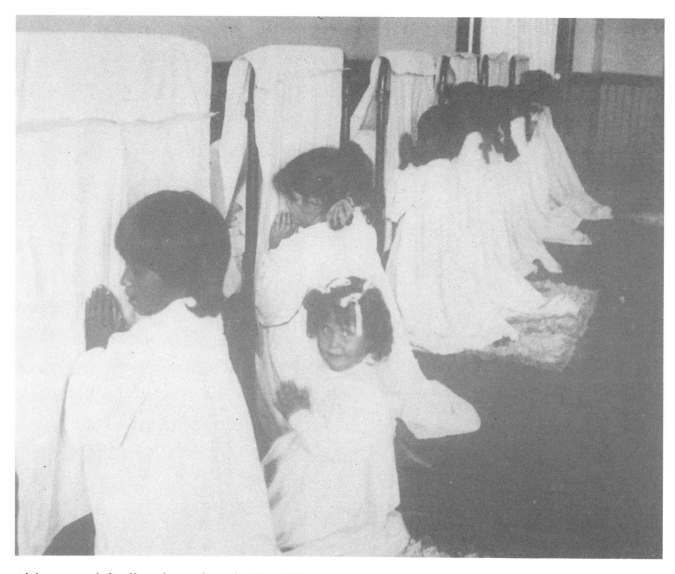

▲ Many Indian children were forced to attend distant boarding schools, often run by Christian missionaries. Sadly, the children were often taught to despise their Indian heritage. They were taught the Christian religion and were often punished if they spoke in their native language instead of English. Here little girls pray by their beds at the Phoenix Indian School in 1900.

Alabama, and finally relocated to the Fort Sill Reservation, in Oklahoma. Later, some of them were allowed to move from Oklahoma to the Mescalero Reservation, where they still live.

The first documented reference to the Navajo was found in a missionary report of 1626. At that time, the Navajo consisted of many small bands who had settled down to become farmers and sheep herders. They also had horses and cattle. It is unclear whether they stole the animals, or obtained them through trade. However, they learned agriculture from the Pueblo.

From their original Southwestern site in the upper San Juan region, the Navajo reached Chaco Canyon. Further west, they settled in Canyon de Chelly in northeastern Arizona around 1700. From Canyon de Chelly the Navajo occasionally raided Spanish settlements until 1805, when the Spanish retaliated. Over 100 Navajo were killed, mostly women, children, and old people. Today the site of the fiercest battle is known as Massacre Cave.

In 1819, the Navajo still living in Canyon de Chelly signed a treaty with the Spanish defining a boundary between the two people. Other treaties came later, but most were soon broken.

Then forts were set up by the United States to control the Navajo, but after the outbreak of the Civil War in 1861, these were abandoned. The

Navajo and Apache raids intensified.

Finally, in 1863, the United States Colonel Kit Carson, known to the Navajo as Red Shirt, entered Canyon de Chelly. He had strict orders to move the Navajo out of the canyon forever. He set his plan into action and destroyed Navajo crops and livestock. Thus, the Navajo were starved into submission. Then 8,000 of them were forced to march 300 miles on foot to be relocated at Fort Sumner in New Mexico. This exhausting trip became known as The Long Walk.

In 1868 the United States signed a treaty allowing the Navajo to return to a 3.5 million acre reservation within their own land. Although the Navajo were overjoyed to be going home, by then everything of value on the land had been destroyed. The Navajo had to start from scratch. Recovery didn't really begin until the government distributed sheep and goats to the Navajo. Today their survival is still based on sheep.

During World War II, about 300 Navajo transmitted secret information in their native language for the United States. These were known as the Navajo Code Talkers. They represented one of the most successful coding projects of the war; theirs was the only war code that was never broken. It substituted over 200 everyday Navajo words for specific military terms.

In 1687 Father Eusebio Kino became the first Spanish missionary to establish headquarters in the Tohono O'odham territory in the hot and arid Southwestern desert. He introduced wheat, chick peas, watermelon, and onions to the Tohono O'odham. He also brought them horses, cattle, and sheep, as well as blankets, calico cloth, medicine, and tools.

Father Kino was also the first Spaniard to meet the Pima. This event took place in 1694. Like the Tohono O'odham, the Pima eventually accepted Father Kino's Christian teachings. Along with the Maricopa, these two tribes acted as guides and allies to help the Spaniards combat the Apache.

In 1853 as part of the Gadsden Purchase, the United States bought land from Mexico upon which about 5,000 Tohono O'odham lived. In 1870, the Pima were given a reservation on the Gila River. Four years later, the Tohono O'odham received a small reservation at San Xavier. They received another parcel of land at Gila Bend in 1883. In 1917, they were given the Sells Reservation, the land where they had always lived.

Most Tohono O'odham, when they speak any language but their own, use Spanish. They have kept their ancient ceremonies, while the Pima's ceremonial life has deteriorated. The Pima also adopted American names and American clothing, and by 1871 they had an American school.

As white settlers, as well as Hualapai and Navajo, moved into their area during the late 19th and early 20th century, bands of Havasupai were forced to forego their informal organization and consolidate in response to the reduction of their territory, and the destruction of much of the natural resources upon which they depended. In 1880 the United States government restricted the Havasupai to a 518-acre reservation within the Grand Canyon. This greatly affected the Havasupai's centuries-old life-style, since they could no longer winter on the snowy plateau surrounding Havasu Canyon. Furthermore, the depletion of resources on the reservation caused many Havasupai to leave their native land in order to make a living. By consolidating, the people were able to establish a formal constitution in 1939. Today, they are represented by an elected tribal council of seven members.

The Havasupai waged a legal battle in the early 1970s to regain the land that had once belonged to them. In 1975 a federal bill was signed into law that established a 160,000 acre reservation, and allotted 95,000 acres of Grand Canyon National Park for the Havasupai's permanent use.

CHANGES IN RESERVATION LIFE

In general, reservation life was hard for the Indians. Disease was rampant and housing was inadequate. Poverty was high and morale was down. The children were sent away to schools where they were taught to speak English and abandon their heritage.

For many decades, things got worse and worse. Then, an important change took place. In 1934 Congress passed the Indian Reorganization Act—a voluntary act—allowing Indians on reservations to draw up formal constitutions and govern themselves through elected tribal councils and officers.

The act proved to be revolutionary. Now Indian heritage could be preserved, their arts encouraged, and their religion replenished. Their pride began to be restored as Indian policies were reformed, and the tribes began setting up their own tribal governments to handle affairs.

▲ R. Carlos Nakai is a well-known modern-day musician and composer, but his flute is unchanged from the type used for many centuries by Southwest Indians.

THE PEYOTE CEREMONY

Peyote is a small spineless cactus that comes from northern Mexico and has been used in rituals first by the Aztec. By eating the dried button-like tops of this plant, the Aztec experienced amazing insights, as well as visions.

Peyote was introduced into the southern Plains in the 1840s. The Lipan Apache were among the first tribes to use it. "Peyote fever" spread, with each Indian tribe adapting their use to fit their cultural background.

As reservation life became harder, a religion formed around the peyote. It signified the importance of being an Indian. It prompted the incorporation of the Native American Church in 1918.

Today, members of the church have peyote ceremonies to celebrate many occasions, from blessing a house to curing an illness. They consider peyote a medicine, not a harmful drug. A peyote chief leads the ceremony. The religion can still be found throughout various Southwestern tribes, including the Tohono O'odham and Navajo. The peyote ceremony includes elements similar to those found in Christian celebrations.

In 1990, a U.S. Supreme Court ruling denied First Amendment protection for peyote use in religious ceremonies. How this affects the Native American Church and its 300,000 members remains to be seen.

SOUTHWEST INDIANS TODAY

The spirit and influence of the Southwestern Indians is strongly felt throughout the region today. Non-Indians and Indians alike can visit many of their ancient sites. They can attend Native American festivals that keep alive the rich traditions. And, there are also many recreational activities now open to the public on reservations.

The 19 pueblos of New Mexico hold public events throughout the year, including many colorful ceremonial dances.

The Zuni Pueblo, with a population of nearly 9,000, is the largest of them all. It is also the only pueblo with its own public school district and its own radio station. Here, you can still see the spectacular Shalako dances every year in late November or early December.

A visit to some of the other pueblos is like a trip back in time, since the people retain many of their old ways, although most homes are now built of cinder blocks. Taos is one of the more famous historic communities, with its people continuing to live in many ways like their ancestors. Acoma is another noteworthy pueblo. It is probably the only village on the Rio Grande that is on the same site it occupied when the Spanish first came.

Today, you can visit the Western Apache if you go to the Fort Apache and San Carlos Reservations in Arizona. Fort Apache has over 25 fine trout-fishing lakes. The White Mountain Apache, a division of the Western Apache, run the Sunrise Resort Park in Whiteriver, Arizona. This is a financially successful motel, restaurant, and ski slope. The tribe also owns a major sawmill, as well as economically thriving fish hatcheries.

The San Carlos Reservation has a water sports area on the land: San Carlos Lake. The tribe also receives income from a second lake, as well as other ponds and streams. The San Carlos Apache have a healthy cattle industry.

The Mescalero Apache live on a reservation in southeast New Mexico. Although their economy has had its ups and downs, today the tribe is financially on solid ground with the tourist complex of the Inn of the Mountain Gods.

The Jicarilla Apache also feature tourist attractions, including eight lakes, on their reservation in northwestern New Mexico. They receive additional income from oil and gas production, and lumber.

In 1989 a non-Indian gave the Chiricahua the deed to land his family owned in southeastern Arizona's Cochise Stronghold Canyon. This land, in the Apache ancestral homeland, is where Cochise had established his fortress against the troopers of the United States Army. On June 8, 1874, Cochise was carried up to a ridge to see the sunrise. This is where he died. Now, for the first time in over a century, the descendants of Cochise and Geronimo once again have property in their traditional lands.

Today, with 200,000 Indians, the Navajo Nation is the largest tribe in the United States. It is also the richest. Oil, coal, uranium, lumber, and livestock have helped the people greatly improve their finances. They live on the Navajo Indian Reservation, which is the size of West Virginia.

The reservation has a tribal zoo, as well as a community college. The campus of Navajo Community College was designed in a traditional eight-sided hogan shape, and the university's Hatathil Museum faces east to honor the traditional beliefs.

The Tribal Council meets at Window Rock,

◀ Pete Zah was elected Navajo tribal chairman for 1983. The natural hole in the mountain behind him gives Window Rock, Arizona, its name. The Navajo tribe has its headquarters here.

the capital of the Navajo Nation, in headquarters decorated by Navajo artist Gerald Naylor. Recently, the council revamped its tribal code to create three separate branches of government, rather than one.

Today, Tohono O'odham live on the Tohono O'odham, San Xavier, Alik Cukson, and Gila Bend reservations in Arizona.

To see their traditional Indian field hockey game, you can attend the annual O'odham Tash Indian Celebration, held at Casa Grande, Arizona, every February. Dancing to Indian bands, as well as a rodeo and arts and craft sales, take place at this time.

The Tohono O'odham also welcome visitors to their annual pageant held at Mission San Xavier del Bac on the Friday following Easter Sunday. San Xavier is a church that was founded in 1700 by Father Kino. It houses the oldest Roman Catholic parish in the United States and still serves the Tohono O'odham people of the San Xavier District.

In 1976 the Tohono O'odham tribe was awarded $26 million by the federal government to settle land and mineral claims. Today, the Tohono O'odham number about 1,000 in Mexico and 25,000 in the United States. After officially changing their name to Tohono O'odham in 1986, they have entered a transition period. While some people prefer the new name, others are more comfortable with the old.

The Tohono O'odham's cousins, the Pima, today live on the Gila River, Salt River, and Alik Cukson reservation in southern Arizona. You can see examples of Pima culture at the Gila River Arts and Crafts Museum in Sacaton, Arizona. Maricopa culture is also represented here, and the Maricopa live on Pima reservations.

The Havasupai Indians now operate two tourist lodges and several campgrounds in the Grand Canyon. This is the last place in the United States where the mail still is carried by

◀ In 1987, controversial government decisions forced Navajo to leave some reservation lands they shared with Hopi Indians in Arizona. Here a group of Hopi elders discusses the problem.

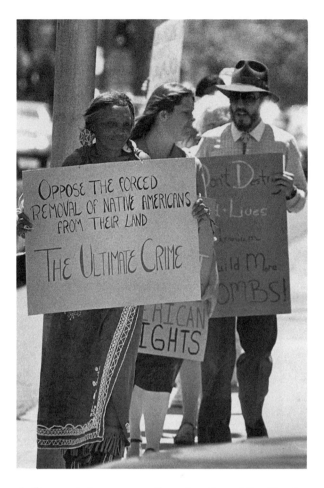

▲ Demonstrators oppose the relocation of the Navajo in northern Arizona in 1987.

mule train.

The Yaqui, whose Easter ceremony is one of Tucson's winter highlights, received 203 acres of federal land about 15 miles southwest of Tucson in 1964. Later, other parcels were added. Then, in 1978 Congress granted the Yaqui status as an official Native American tribe. This makes the people eligible to receive federal money for health, housing, social service, and education programs. Today, the tribe has about 5,600 members in the United States and 30,000 in Sonora, Mexico. Many Yaqui prefer being referred to as Yoeme, meaning person.

While Indians of the Southwest are faced with many problems, they are also becoming more aware of how to work within the law to get what they need. Tribal organizations strive to bring new pride to the young and to keep the old traditions alive, while helping the people live in a rapidly changing world.

▲ Navajo Community College is located in the Four Corners area of the Navajo reservation. Most of the buildings on the campus are in the shape of hogans, the traditional, round Navajo dwelling. The building shown here is the Ned Hatathli Culture Center.

▲ A Navajo family in traditional dress gathers at the door of its hogan.

◀ A school on the Havasupai Reservation in Arizona. In 1975, the Havasupai regained some of their ancestral lands on the South Rim of the Grand Car on.

▼ A Native American works to restore ruins at Gran Quivira, an abandoned pueblo with a mission church, in Salinas National Monument, New Mexico. The inhabitants of all of the Salinas villages eventually left the area for Rio Grande Valley pueblos and El Paso.

▲ A beautifully decorated traditional pottery jar rests near a doorway at Taos Pueblo.

▼ Taos Pueblo, near Taos, New Mexico, looks today much as it did centuries ago, though some homes now have electricity.

▶ A wood fire burns in an above-ground beehive oven in Taos Pueblo. These ovens were introduced to the Indians by the Spanish.

▲ Ceremonial life was very important to Southwest Indians, as it is to their descendants today. This Navajo boy is shown in his handsome ceremonial costume.

INDEX

PICTURE CREDITS

Stewart Aitchison: 18, 19, 89, 90; Arizona Office of Tourism: 16, 22 top; Atlatl: 69 top, 70; Bandelier National Monument: 66; Canyon Records Productions (John Running): 84; Richard Day: 48; L.A. Jansen: 17, 92 top and bottom; Library of Congress: 6, 15, 26, 27, 30, 31 top and bottom, 32, 33 left, 34, 35 right, 39, 51 right, 53, 54, 55, 57, 58, 61, 64, 75, 79, 81; Ed McCombs: 88; Mesa Verde National Park: 20 top and bottom, 21; Robert and Linda Mitchell: 41 bottom, 45 bottom, 47, 68 bottom; Montezuma Castle National Monument: 13; Museum of Northern Arizona: 65 top, 65 bottom (Marc Gaede), 67 (Christy Turner III), 71 top ID# NA3288.32 (Marc Gaede), 71 bottom (Marc Gaede); National Archives of the United States: contents page, 8, 9, 12, 28, 29, 33 right, 35 left, 36, 37, 38, 40, 51 left, 52, 56, 59, 60, 62 left and right, 63 left and right, 74, 76, 77, 78, 80, 82; Jack Olson: 22 bottom, 23, 24, 44; Pecos National Historical Park: 10-11; Jeffrey Rich: 46; Chase Roe: 94; Eda Rogers: 69 bottom; Saguaro National Monument: 42, 43 top and bottom; Sylvia Schlender: 68 top, 91; C.M. Slade: 93; Scott T. Smith: 41 top, 45 top; United States Postal Service: 72; UPI/Bettmann: 86 top and bottom, 87.

979
LIP

Liptak, Karen.

Indians of the
Southwest.

20825

DATE			